Armchair Traveller
at the bookHaus

Baja California, in modern-day Mexico, is one of the longest peninsulas in the world, and certainly one of the most geographically diverse. Pino Cacucci travels through endless expanses of desert, salt mountains and rows of cacti with thorns so sharp they can impale thirsty birds; he rediscovers local traditions and old legends of queens and giant pearls. Cacucci also explores the breathtaking coastal areas, where whales play alongside fishing boats. Sixty years ago, Mexico became the first country to create a safe haven for whales, and even today these enigmatic animals seem to understand that it is possible for humans and animals to live in harmony.

The Whales Know
A Journey Through Mexican California

Pino Cacucci

Translated by Katherine Gregor

Armchair Traveller
at the bookHaus

First published as *Le balene lo sanno* in April 2009 by
Giangiacomo Feltrinelli Editore, Milan, Italy

First published in Great Britain in 2013 by The Armchair Traveller at the
bookHaus, 70 Cadogan Place, London SW1X 9AH

A CIP catalogue record for this book can be found at the British Library

Print ISBN: 978-1-907973-88-8
Ebook ISBN: 978-1-907973-93-2

Typeset in Garamond by MacGuru Ltd
info@macguru.org.uk

Printed in China by 1010 Printing International Ltd

A land of wonders and mirages.
Your eyes penetrate it with an unsure step.
Nothing here is as it seems.

GABRIEL TRUJILLO MUÑOZ

Contents

'Call Me Ishmael'

HER NAME WAS *BLACK WARRIOR*. She was a whaler launched from the dockyards of Duxbury, Massachusetts in 1825. For over a quarter of a century, she slaughtered cetaceans in the Pacific and Indian Oceans. Finally, in 1858, she was purchased by a Honolulu shipping magnate and the new crew headed south, to that part of California which still belonged to Mexico after the Mexican-American War of 1846–8. The captain knew that in that huge bay between the Vizcaino Desert in the east and Isla Cedros in the west, there lay a vast sheltered lagoon where thousands of grey whales converged from the Arctic seas, in order to give birth and mate. The place was known as Ojo de Liebre – 'Hare Spring', a name given by the natives to a freshwater spring that flows at the east end – which had been 'discovered' only a year earlier by the most infamous whale hunter of all time, Charles Melville Scammon, who by a trick of fate partly shared a name with the author of *Moby Dick*. Even now, the caption 'Scammon's Lagoon' appears on US nautical maps, whereas in Spanish language areas Mr Scammon appears almost always alongside the epithet *infame depredador de ballenas*, 'infamous whale predator'. Within the space of just a few years, Scammon and his followers killed so many grey whales they reduced their population to a few hundred, whereas in previous decades there had been estimated to be at least 20,000. At the beginning of the 20th century the grey whale was declared 'extinct'. Fortunately that was wrong, and did not take into account the role Mexico would take on as a guardian of natural equilibrium – the first country to do so.

On 10 December 1858 the butchering was only too easy: all you had to do was strike a defenceless newborn, and the mother would try to rescue it before falling prey herself to the harpoons. *Black Warrior* caused a massacre: the waters of the Laguna Ojo de Liebre were red with blood, the men aboard were breathless from all the heaving and cutting, separating the fat and melting it in cauldrons to transform it into precious oil, loading barrels into the hold and throwing the carcasses back into the sea. It was the greed of those whalers that spelt the demise of the ship: because of the excessive weight she ran aground in shallow waters at the exit of the cove; the hull split and the prow sank. She remained with the stern up in the air, displaying the name fishermen were to read for years to come: *Black Warrior*. It became a reference point and a sign of danger for whoever sailed across the 28th Parallel North, which passes right there, and someone even took the trouble of translating it into Spanish: Guerrero Negro. Meanwhile, grey whales had disappeared from the North Atlantic and from the Japanese and Korean coasts, and those that populated the Arctic seas were being decimated during their annual migration to Baja California. This went on until 1946, when Mexico banned hunting in its territorial waters, allowing for a slow but steady repopulation. In 1971 it granted the status of 'sanctuary' to the three bays where whales converge from the Bering Sea. These bays became the world's first protected reservations for cetaceans. And when the layer of desert between the Pacific and the Sea of Cortez started to be exploited for its salt pans, the village that sprang up there was named Guerrero Negro. Nowadays, Guerrero Negro is a town that has grown along the main road and which exists for two reasons: its salt, which is exported to three continents, and the influx of tourists from January to March, drawn by the experience of an emotionally moving contact with thousands of grey whales.

We are on the 28th Parallel North exactly halfway down Baja California, one of the world's longest peninsulas. Almost 2,000 kilometres of the Carretera Federal Mexico 1 zig-zags through various locations, from one coast to the other, crossing the Vizcaino Desert: cacti as far as the eye can see, a strip of asphalt heading straight towards infinity, with the occasional bend suddenly revealing tableaux of bays rendered magical by white sand. As we approach Guerrero Negro, I am struck by the sight of fields in bloom: the desert turns into a garden. The night's moisture produces miracles and the irrigation allows you to admire these green fields that are almost an oasis in comparison to what you witnessed a moment earlier. A little further down you see another leap from one extreme to the other: entering the salt pans is like descending into a lunar landscape. Two hundred and sixty square kilometres of blinding whiteness with endless 'basins', which, depending on the moment, take on a purple hue or turn iridescent pink. You see monsters of orange steel; huge Dart Trucks that carry 500 tonnes of salt in every load, and a maze of runways as wide as those of an international airport, where without an expert guide you would vanish into thin air. 'It used to happen a lot,' I am told by Roberto de la Fuente, who has worked in the salt pans half his life, 'When visitors used to be allowed in without restrictions. Every so often, the old Dakota would take off and fly over the area, looking for missing people. Now that production has reached 20,000 tonnes a day that would be too dangerous. Just consider that those things,' he says, pointing at vehicles with tyres ten times larger than those of an articulated lorry, 'Need at least 300 metres in order to brake. So basically they don't brake if they see an obstacle. It happened a while back to a technician who'd got off the pick-up to test the salt levels. On the way back all he could see was the roof of his pick-up completely razed to the ground; the whole van was now 10 centimetres thick. What do you Italians call it? That's right, it was as flat as a pizza.'

Roberto now works for Malarrímo, the agency that organises visits to Guerrero Negro and to Laguna Ojo de Liebre. Malarrímo is the name of a famous beach, well known not for bathing, but for the currents which throw ashore anything they happen to pick up along the Pacific coast, flowing past Japan and then going back down along the American continent – those same natural routes that were used by Spanish galleons returning to Acapulco from the Philippines. The name is difficult to explain: the verb *arrimar* means 'to come alongside,' and *a mal arrímo* is, in this case, an unfortunate way to end up on the coast. In other words, it is a place where you get thrown in spite of your best intentions – for instance, after a shipwreck. You can find all sorts of things on that beach, including satellite fragments, aerial targets and the odd torpedo that requires the bomb disposal unit to check if it is still live or spent. The Hotel Malarrímo has maritime paraphernalia hanging from walls and ceilings – it is almost like an archaeological museum that contains not only pieces of wing and fuselage from military aircraft from the 'modern' era, but also 19th-century harpoons and, naturally, whale bones. Moreover, there are countless bottles containing the oddest messages.

Malarrímo could not miss out on the sailing ducks. Their epic journey began on 10 January 1992, when a Chinese merchant ship en route from Hong Kong to the US ran into a storm and lost three containers full of rubber ducks – at least 28,000 of them – the ones you float to entertain the children at bath time. It is a form of pollution, since they are practically indestructible for decades, if not centuries. However, Seattle oceanographer Curtis Ebbesmeyer decided to launch a worldwide appeal for sightings of the errant ducks, with a view to studying currents. Some of them deviated south, others were pushed towards the Bering Strait at the speed of a mile a day and a few ended up on the coast of Britain.

Moreover, the company in Tacoma that was supposed to receive them in the first place pledged $100 for every recovered duck, unleashing a collectors' race and a delirium that sees some of them with a price tag of up to 700 euros on eBay. Those that landed in Malarrímo, bleached and useless, are mixed up with a pile of other caked, corroded and unusable toys.

As we reach the quay, fish eagles brush the surface of the lagoon and grab fish with their talons – flashes of silver reflect on Guerrero Negro's permanently grey sky, even though it hardly ever rains here: that is why the salt dries up in this microclimate, which is unique in the world. Fish eagles usually build their nests on top of electricity poles: in the past few years, people have decided to build a sort of extra wooden shelf on top of the poles, to stop the birds of prey from causing problems to the electrical network and from being electrocuted. Every so often, the eagles pick a strange place, like the top of a draining pipe or the bucket of a digger. 'In such cases,' the old hand Roberto assures me, 'the machine is just left there until the chicks are old enough to fly. Here, fish eagles are as highly respected as grey whales: no matter what they choose to do, we fit around them. This is also because Baja California has very strict laws where the environment is concerned.'

There is a noisy eaglet poking out of every nest. Its parents, out on patrol, respond to its cries whilst circling majestically above. It is the seagulls that turn out to be the only 'dangerous' birds: the roof of Roberto's van is covered in dents caused by *almejas catarinas* – large shells the seagulls grab with their talons and then drop from a considerable height in order to crack them. If an *almeja* lands on your head you are guaranteed concussion at the very least.

Javier, the boatman, welcomes us aboard. As soon as he pulls away from the quay, he turns on the gas and the motorboat takes off, shooting towards the middle of Laguna Ojo de Liebre. After an hour's journey, Javier turns the powerful engine down to a minimum. The sea is the colour of steel and the cold seeps into your bones – something you could not have imagined a moment ago, in the tropical climate of the 28th Parallel North. Only a few metres away from our boat rises a powerful sigh, like a muffled breath, and the spray from the blowhole dampens our faces. It comes very close to us and now the glossy tail stands erect before immersion. Even closer this time, an enormous head emerges, covered in incrustations. It stands just like that, upright, for ten seconds or so, observing us. Then, with surprising agility, it leaps sideways and dives: 14 metres of tapered bulk weighing 40 tonnes, making a gigantic splash.

Within half an hour, we are surrounded by dozens of playful and merry grey whales: it is the most emotionally overwhelming experience you can have in Baja California – a patch of land that has no equal in terms of unforgettable sensations. After all, it is not just a question of 'sighting' the grey whales but of joking with them, of touching them, of being the object of their curiosity and even their pranks. One of them is lying on its side and using its fin to scoop water onto the tourists in another boat until they are well and truly soaked: their joyous cries and laughter confirm to the giant that its mission has been accomplished. Mothers push their 'little ones' – they weigh half a tonne at birth – towards us, in order, as Javier explains, to get them used to humans, so that when they return next year, as 'adolescents', they will have built up some confidence. Some of them play a game which can be a little scary at first: they prop up the keel with their backs, lift up the motorboat and carry it forward quickly for a few hundred metres. In all these years there has never been an accident. Never has a whale capsized a boat through 'excessive enthusiasm'.

'They know exactly what they're doing and they do it gently,' expert-boatman Javier assures us. For nine years now he has been best friends with these cetaceans, who are so affectionate towards our less-than-deserving species.

So why do they do it, then? Why do they have this insuppressible instinct, this yearning for friendship with human beings, to the point of practically showing off their offspring by lifting them up and coming close to the boats, while the offspring, like oversized playful kittens, allow themselves to be stroked and even kissed by the more emotional female tourists of the party? How is it that after they were slaughtered for centuries – and some are still being slaughtered (by the Japanese and, to a lesser extent, by the Norwegians and Icelanders, not to mention the Russians whose actions are not fully known) – the whales seem to know that here in Mexico they have had nothing to fear for over half a century? Experts on the subject claim that the world's largest mammals are instinctively attracted to those other mammals who carried on living on the earth's crust while they chose to return to the sea where everything originated. Who knows? I like to think that they are intelligent enough to tell the difference: that on the coast of Baja California, humans are friendly. And there is no doubt they most definitely know that. In any case, these are grey whales, *Eschrichtius robustus*, who distinguish themselves by this playful behaviour, while other species are cautious and only socialise occasionally. They are also the mammals that migrate the furthest – a return journey of 20,000 kilometres between the Bering Sea and Baja California. It is a traveller's life, organised by the perfect number – three. They spend three months in Arctic waters feeding and building up fat and energy, then three months swimming, and another three courting mates in the three areas of Baja California that are their sanctuaries – Ojo de Liebre, San Ignacio and Bahía Magdalena – or for those who got pregnant the year before, giving birth and nursing. Then, finally, three months are spent travelling back to the northern glaciers – glaciers which, until recently, were termed eternal; but now, *quién sabe?*

We know very little about them: we know that they communicate with one another across huge distances, though we do not quite understand how on earth they propagate sounds; we know that they navigate by the sun and the earth's magnetic field; that they are able to echolocate in order to survey the ocean floor; that they are sociable and gregarious and live in communities, and that if ever one of them is harpooned, the others will try to rescue it, putting themselves at risk of being hit. Moreover, their tendency to be so incredibly friendly, which we witness here in Laguna Ojo de Liebre, is not always so: if a mother sees her offspring being killed, she will attack. In the 19th century, there were various cases of brigantines sunk by head-butting grey whales blinded by grief, who would commit suicide while dragging the murderers down to the bottom. That is why the grey whale earned the nickname 'devil fish' from English-speaking whalers who mistook the largest of mammals for a 'fish'. Among themselves, whales have no hierarchy, but a sort of mutual aid system, as well as defence roles. For example, the entrance to the lagoon from the open sea is patrolled in turn by the young ones eager to learn, as well as the stronger males – seasoned 'warriors' – and they prevent killer whales and sharks from entering and slaughtering the little ones. They organise a sort of beat system and take it in turns to keep watch while the infants suckle about 40 litres' worth per feed, peaceful and protected.

If the friendly grey whales can become aggressive when they see their loved ones killed, they are, nevertheless, among the most harmless of creatures where humans are concerned; contrary to the sperm whale, which is larger and more powerful – a predator always ready to put up a mighty fight. There is a legend about a sperm whale that inspired Moby Dick – the 'white whale' in Herman Melville's novel which opens with the almost mythical line, 'Call me Ishmael'. '[...] A noble Sperm Whale in the full majesty of his might.' That sperm whale really did exist: the whalers called him Mocha Dick because he engaged in his first battle in front of Mocha Island in the Chiloé Archipelago, off the coast of Chile, in 1810.

He was lighter in colour than other sperm whales, a silvery grey, and back then already had a long white scar running across his head. Twenty-two metres long, proud and indomitable, he had escaped harpooners by head-butting longboats and capsizing them. Who knows what else he did until his next recorded appearance, 30 years later, and what feats he undertook.

He resurfaces in sailors' memories in 1840: an English whaler sighted him in the Australian Pacific. The watch cried out the usual warning, 'There she blows!' to indicate the vapour spray of the blowholes, and two longboats with hunters were lowered. They rowed and rowed, and the closer they got, the more their anxiety grew. There was no mistaking him. Mocha Dick, the largest sperm whale they had ever seen, seemed to calculate the distances; he wore them out during the chase, and managed to dodge the harpoons by just a few metres each time. Finally, he dived abruptly, only to head-butt even more powerfully from below. Smashed to pieces, the first longboat went straight down. The sailors were tossed up into the air and came falling back down into the water. While the second boat was rescuing the survivors, Mocha Dick renewed his attack, and this time opened his enormous mouth wide, sank his rows of large, fanged teeth into the longboat, and crunched it.

This is not just a legend. It was not merely the fruit of long storytelling sessions during the tedium of waiting aboard during endless crossings. We need only remember that in the 19th century and even earlier, sperm whales that weighed up to 65 tonnes would kill dozens of whalers every year, and many men returned maimed to the harbour and spent the rest of their days telling their drama over and over again in taverns, surrounded by the indifference of the other drinkers.

The whalers allegedly sighted Mocha Dick's scarred head a month later. The harpooners had just killed a female sperm whale and were dragging her towards the ship to haul her aboard and cut her up when Mocha Dick rushed at them.

Once he had destroyed the longboat, he went up to the dead whale and, before the eyes of the dumbfounded crew, ignored the survivors and began pushing the lifeless carcass, maybe imagining at first that he was saving what had probably been his mate. Then, resigned, he took her far away just to stop her from being taken by his 'enemies'.

Subsequent sightings of Mocha Dick blend into legend and all that is known for certain is that his life came to an end in 1859. It was not old age and accumulated exhaustion that got the better of him, but his generous bond with his fellow creatures: once again, he rushed at a whaleboat to try to rescue other whales that had been harpooned. At this point, accounts differ. According to some texts, it was a Swedish ship, while the Chilean writer Luis Sepúlveda claims that it was a Basque whaler under the command of Captain Ignacio Etchevarría. Sepúlveda not only knew the story of that sperm whale very well but was also a close friend of the great storyteller Francisco Coloane, a native of the Chiloé Archipelago, of which Mocha Island was a part, and a troubadour who related its numerous tales. The old sperm whale lived up to his reputation: harpooned through the lung, he began bleeding copiously until, exhausted, he lay still on the ocean surface. The harpooners approached to retrieve him, ready to finish him off. However, like in an adventure story, Mocha Dick was merely pretending to be dead: as soon as the first boat was within reach of his tail, he dealt a blow that sent it flying through the air, killing more sailors, before being killed himself by harpoons thrown from surrounding longboats.

The ship that killed him announced that she had avenged Mocha Dick's 'victims'. The ship butchers, besides being astounded by the countless scars, extracted from his flesh at least 19 old harpoon points. The indomitable sperm whale who never fled, but on the contrary, counterattacked, did not know that eight years earlier, he had inspired a great writer to write a memorable novel. And who knows if Meville ever came to know that the real Moby Dick had fallen in battle, without understanding the reason for all this hatred, but just reacting instinctively to the aggression? At the time, the New York writer was devoting himself to poetry and travel memoirs, to Shakespearean reflections on appearance and reality and all the while hiding behind anonymity to flee from fame, which he disliked. It was only five years later, in 1864, that the epic of whalers who risked their lives and whales ready to put up a fight would come to an abrupt end; the Norwegian captain Svend Foyn, who was accustomed to slaughtering seals rather than cetaceans, invented the exploding harpoon. It was a cannon with a 50-metre range that shot a device with five hooks that opened on impact with the victim's body, breaking a phial of sulphuric acid which then triggered a charge of gunpowder. The explosion inside the flesh would kill the whale instantly – or almost. The chase would then be entrusted to the new steam vessels, which were much faster than sailing ships. Nowadays, killing whales is like murdering children in a nursery school: radars, laser aiming systems, turbine engines, workshops on board the ships to perform the slaughtering, sighting helicopters that take off from the helipad on the upper deck. Modern instruments for an ancient crime. There is no need that could justify it; it is no more than a whim on the part of a few.

Thanks to the explosive harpoon, just as I write this, there is news that calls into question the theories on the average age of whales – 80 years more or less, though some live to 100, depending on the species. An old specimen killed by Inuits had a harpoon embedded in it with a US-manufactured charge produced between 1870 and 1880, which had failed to explode at the time. Therefore, that poor whale must have been at least 140 years old, probably even older, considering the fact that it must already have been an adult when the harpoon was planted. As for the Inuits who put an end to the long life of this great old man of the sea, whose experiences made up an extraordinary heritage, they devote themselves to this 'pastime' more out of a sense of tradition than true necessity. I keep thinking of the native communities in Chiapas, who speak an enlightening truth: there are good traditions worth preserving, and pernicious traditions from which we need to free ourselves. Is it not high time that the Inuits – who use snowmobiles, put highly polluting antifreeze in the radiators of huge jeeps, have radios, televisions and even refrigerators – dropped 'traditions' they should be ashamed of? After all, on the occasions when they kill a whale it is just to organise a sort of ritualistic celebration at which they eat just a tiny piece of meat, then throw the rest into the sea.

Going back to mid-18th-century sailing ships, Captain Ahab's *Pequod* was a very similar vessel to the *Black Warrior* that ran aground in front of Laguna Ojo de Liebre. It had three masts with lugsails, and a hold capacious enough to contain a large number of oil barrels. It was heavy and slow but sturdy enough to withstand storms, and equipped with a reinforced keel able to break through newly formed ice crusts, even though this could be a nightmare for whalers, since getting trapped in the ice meant certain death. In the case of the *Black Warrior* and the *Pequod*, the hull was lighter and therefore swifter, because unlike the English, the Americans of the whaling fleet based in the harbours of Nantucket and New Bedford seldom went hunting as far as the Antarctic.

We return in the early afternoon: sailing in Laguna Ojo de Liebre is permitted only from 8 a.m. to 3 p.m. It is forbidden to disturb the whales outside these times. We skirt around the huge sand Isla Arena, which is in fact formed of dunes and is uninhabited but populated by a wide variety of bird species. A flock of sea lions is crowding a large buoy. The males roar and open their mouths wide: the entire act is for the benefit of their harem.

At night in Guerrero Negro, which owes its name to the *Black Warrior* and which supplanted the massacres with a tourism industry for Mother Nature lovers, the wind howls and roars, raising clouds of sand and salt. Our hotel is situated exactly on the 28th Parallel North, which is also the border between two states of the Mexican Federation – Baja California Sur and Baja California 'Norte'. Naturally, it is not a question of crossing borders, as such, but there is a kind of motorway toll booth, a sort of sentry box used specifically to control the goods carried by articulated lorries coming from the north: Baja Sur is proud to be immune to plant infestations widespread elsewhere, and takes care to safeguard that immunity. Owing to a whim of the geography of the Carretera Federal 1, our hotel is situated in Baja Sur, but in order to gain entrance, you need to travel about 100 metres into Baja California. Our Dodge Durango crosses this 'border' two or three times a day, and since the 'customs officers' change between dawn and dusk, every time I pass I get asked where I am going, where I come from and what I am transporting.

2

Return to La Paz

THIS TIME, I have travelled around the peninsula of Baja California in the reverse direction to the one I took ten years ago, when I landed in San Diego then went from the Tijuana border down almost 2,000 kilometres to Cabo San Lucas, the golden finis terrae, an amusement centre full of bars, discos and massive hotels, with lots of concrete and very little of authentic Mexico. Though naturally, you cannot ignore the splendid beaches and that arch of rock immortalised by so many advertisements. I also know that Jacques Cousteau, a regular visitor to these shores, discovered an underwater canyon a few miles from the coast that is larger than the Grand Canyon, where millions of tonnes of sand moved by currents slide down underwater cliffs to then fall into the abyss. It is practically as large as Niagara Falls, but in reverse: sand instead of water, and water instead of air. I would be able to see all of this with a bathyscaphe like the one on the *Calypso*. Instead, on the outside, I can see, and especially hear, the frenetic throbbing of a non-city that is at odds with the peaceful tranquillity of the rest of the peninsula. That is why I have decided to start my journey in La Paz, the discreet and calm capital of Baja Sur, where I have rediscovered a custom unknown to Italian cities: you need only but hint with your foot that you are about to step down from the pavement and the traffic stops as if by magic. The motorists observe you, trying to assess whether or not you are about to cross, and at times, I have crossed the road just so as not to disappoint them. It is just one of the many details that make Baja a quiet and welcoming place, with a relaxed pace of life, scarcely populated and with small, man-sized – as opposed to car-sized – cities where many US citizens and Canadians either spend the winter or settle permanently.

La Paz was the first attempt at a Spanish settlement in this region. Conquistador Hernán Cortés came this far in 1535, lured by the then plentiful pearls just a few metres under-water in the bay. For centuries, pearls represented a source of wealth for exploitative foreign companies, providing hardship and nothing but crumbs for the *buzos*, fishermen who would dive without a scaphander diving suit. Finally, around 1940, underwater technology supplied the means to polish them off completely, and pearl oysters disappeared, as though wiped out by an epidemic.

Once he had conquered Tenochtitlán, the capital of the Aztec empire, Cortés noticed an abundance of pearls among the looted treasures. When questioned about them, the defeated Aztecs told stories that always mentioned the North and its coastline as the place of origin of this wealth. Above all, Cortés must have read the chivalric novel, *Las Sergas de Esplandián* by Garci Rodríguez de Montalvo, sequel to the successful *Amadís de Gaula*. The latter, published in Seville in 1510, was a book relating the adventures of the hero Esplandián, and had enjoyed unequalled success in Spain at the time. To show just how popular it was, Bernal Díaz de Castillo, chronicler in the retinue of the Mexican expedition, refers to Rodríguez de Montalvo's work when trying to illustrate the wonders of Tenochtitlán, describing it as 'a magical legend', and Cervantes quotes it in his *Don Quixote* – with a hint of irony, since it was because of similar adventure novels that the Knight of the Sad Countenance embarked on such eccentric feats. By a singular twist of fate, an island called California featured in the book – a realm of Amazons led by

Queen Calafia, as beautiful as she is proud and bellicose. In the book, Esplandían flirts with Calafia and the legend of the pearls that adorned the Amazon queen's naked body seems too strange to be a coincidence.

Cortés was now a pragmatic man of 48, not suggestible, but probably lured by such coincidences. In any case, the evidence provided by the Aztecs pushed him in that direction. In 1533, he decided to launch an expedition to the Pacific coast, on board the *Concepción*, under the command of Diego de Becerra, and the *San Lázaro*, under Captain Hernando de Grijalva. They set sail from Manzanillo on 30 October, and a couple of months later the two ships went their separate ways. The *San Lázaro* sailed the open seas, and upon discovering the Revillagigedo Archipelago, returned to the coast to wait in vain for the other ship at the appointed place. In the meantime, there had been a mutiny on board the *Concepción*. The second mate, Fortún Ximénez, had slit the captain's throat in his sleep and taken command of the ship. It is not clear whether this was because of an old grudge, or whether the conditions imposed by the victim had been tyrannical, or if, most probably, the mutineer Fortún was too greedy to share the pearls with Cortés. In fact, the *Concepción* followed along the coastline and the new captain went into the Gulf of California and landed in the bay of La Paz, convinced that it was an island. They were welcomed by a native community living there, the Guaycuras, who spoke a language the Spaniards did not understand since they were only used to the Nahuatl of the Aztecs and to various Mayan dialects of Mexico's Atlantic coast. The Guaycuras were friendly, lived in peace and did not use war to conquer new territories. They fished, hunted and picked fruit. To them, the bearded men from the sea presented no threat. Later, Spanish chronicles of the time would mention 'men who had been too long at sea, and saw half-naked Indian women.' In fact, the mutinous followers of Fortún de Jiménez raped every woman in sight. Although the Guaycuras were peaceful, they were skilful with bows and arrows. They were good huntsmen, and shot the invaders one by one, and even Fortún ended up like a pin cushion. Only a few Spaniards escaped the massacre and managed to reach the *Concepción*, and a few weeks later landed on the coast of Jalisco. There, they were captured by the guards of another conquistador, the notorious Nuño de Guzmán. Before being hanged, they were forced to talk. Their tales strongly confirmed the existence of the pearls and it is possible that, in an attempt to save their skins, they may have embellished the legend of the Amazon Island.

This time, Cortés chose to go in person, and in 1536 he arrived in that very bay, which he called Santa Cruz, and which is now known as La Paz. He managed to collect only a few pearls, and his attempt to set up a colony failed miserably: the hostility of the Indios – who had learnt from previous experience – and the forbidding conditions of an arid and torrid land persuaded him to give up by the beginning of the following year. The history of La Paz would become nothing but a succession of failed attempts and natural disasters that made a fool of him: he hardly knew any respite. The bay was razed to the ground more than once by *chubascos* - tropical hurricanes that batter the Sea of Cortés, a useful starting point for Spanish reprisals against the Indios - and then half destroyed by the latter's counterattacks. La Paz also became an outpost for privateers who attacked galleons entering the gulf in order to restock on drinking water. Then there was the climate: the heat of the long summer months was so stifling that it gave rise to the most credible version of the origin of the name 'California'; according to Jesuit historiographer Clavijero, the same Cortés, eager to show off his Latin, had described the 'island' as a *callida fornax* ('hot furnace'). However, since the name 'California' already featured in Montalvo's book of chivalric feats published in 1510, this version of events becomes less satisfactory. Even so, the term underwent changes over the centuries because according to some scholars, Montalvo took it from *La Chanson de*

Roland, an 11th-century poem of chivalric feats. In it, one of the nations cursed by Charlemagne in retaliation against the murder of his faithful champion in Roncesvalles, was 'the people of Califerna.' This is a detail that brings to mind many 'howlers' taken from literature and then inserted into history. In fact, during the battle at Roncesvalles, on 15 August 778, it was not the 'Saracens,' or Muslims who slaughtered the rearguard led by Roland, but the Basques. But, in the words of Moustache in *Irma La Douce*, that is another story.

In La Paz, legends about pirates continue to blossom, attracting treasure hunters whose expeditions remain cloaked in a fog of voices, rumours, assertions that are impossible to prove, sudden riches automatically afflicted by curses and so forth. One definite fact is that this bay bore witness to some of the most notorious privateers of the 16th and 17th centuries. Privateers – not pirates.

Authentic piracy spread mainly in the Sea of the Antilles, especially the Caribbean, and only sporadically in the Pacific. In Europe, apart from Muslim predators who were privateers thanks to the support of the Turks, the one and only pirate was arguably Klaus Störtebeker who, in 1400, attacked ships of the Hanseatic League in the Baltic and at the mouth of Elba, and founded a brotherhood of free men, inspired by a kind of manifesto that advocated the pursuit of happiness. His feats are celebrated in a beautiful story by Luis Sepúlvida, in his collection *Las Rosas de Atacama*.

Pirates were therefore free men at war with all powers, who indiscriminately attacked ships flying any flag and who had instituted a rule of self-discipline based on mutual aid and the equal sharing of loot. In some ways, the pirates of the Caribbean were anarchists ahead of their time, fought by every contemporary fleet and standing proudly against every one of them. They turned Tortuga Island into a legendary starting point for their raids and formed a kind of association – the Coast Brothers – whose membership included sailors from various countries, notably England, France and Holland. That embryonic libertarian society was an example of 'democracy' during an era of absolutism and fanaticism, where decisions were taken by a vote and assemblies were held where nobody was ever denied the right to voice his opinion. Pirates of the Sea of the Antilles were also known as buccaneers, from the French *boucan*, the grill they used for smoking meat, back in the days when they were poachers rather than adventurers of the seven seas.

When electing the captain aboard a pirate vessel, a cabin boy's vote was equal to that of the bosun. A unique but not infrequent characteristic of the times was that women enjoyed considerable freedom at the base, and even though the crew aboard a ship was always exclusively male, there were cases of female pirates who took command or fought alongside their companions. In his *A General History of the Pyrates*, Daniel Defoe dedicates a whole chapter to Mary Read, born in England in 1690, who wore female clothes while sailing in the Caribbean but would dress as a man when attacking another ship. For a time, she was joined by another famous Irish 'lady pirate,' Anne Bonny. They were forever linked by adverse fortune: in 1720, their vessel, under the command of the notorious Calico Jack Rackham, was attacked by an English frigate that was more powerful both in terms of weapons and in crew size. One by one, the men all fell in the deadly broadside of artillery and the burst of muskets from the naval infantry, until there were only three people left fighting on deck: Calico Jack, Mary Read and Anne Bonny. Out of ammunition and exhausted, the women dropped their swords and were captured. They were about to be hanged, when they were discovered to be pregnant. British law forbade the hanging of pregnant women, so while Calico Jack swung, the two women were locked up in a cell. They say Anne Bonny was hanged the following year, while Mary Read died from an infection during childbirth. However, another legend has it that they both escaped and went back to romping around the Sea of the Antilles under the black banner bearing the skull and crossbones.

In reality privateers were mercenaries in the pay of the Crown of England, or sometimes Holland, authorised by a 'Letter of Marque' to attack Spanish galleons. The most famous among them was undoubtedly Sir Francis Drake, who earnt himself the title of baronet thanks to the huge quantity of Spanish treasures he plundered on both the oceans that flank the Americas. He was also a great sailor who, thanks to his knowledge of the Strait of Magellan, managed to escape the storms at Cape Horn. Drake was a frequent visitor to Baja California, and landed many times in Pichilingue, a sheltered cove next to the bay of La Paz. The term corsair (from the Latin *cursarius*, meaning pirate), is derived from the privateering licences granted by British monarchs, masters at the sly art of dealing a blow but then playing the innocent. Since they did not wish to enter openly into a conflict with Spain, they gave free rein to the best soldier-sailors, such as Sir Walter Raleigh, who was 'intimate' with Elizabeth I – they called him her 'favourite' at the time – so as to render trade between Mexico and the Philippines on the Pacific as difficult as possible, and prevent riches from reaching the coast of Spain, across the Atlantic.

Another English privateer who pillaged numerous Spanish galleons was Sir Thomas Cavendish. He sailed from Plymouth in 1586, in possession of a privateering licence signed by Queen Elizabeth, followed along the Argentinean Patagonia coastline, beyond the Strait of Magellan, then up the Pacific coast, pillaging colonies with inadequate garrisons until he reached Baja California. There he lurked, staging highly profitable ambushes. Galleons sailing from Acapulco – the most important commercial harbour of its day in the Pacific – would reach Manila after only a month, thanks to favourable winds. However, they took four months on their way back, because of the Kuro Siwo stream, which laps the coast of Japan, then goes down the coast of America. Otherwise, sailing on the wind would have taken much longer, especially if we consider just how heavy and slow these floating giants must have been. Even so, the streams prevented them from straying far from the coast and that made them easy prey for the swift and light sailing ships commanded by expert privateers like Drake and Cavendish. The latter, after filling his hold with gold and fine merchandise, continued sailing towards the Mariana Islands and the Philippines, reached the Moluccas and Java, circumnavigated the Cape of Good Hope, and then returned to base. It was a round-the-world trip of two years and 50 days that earnt him the nickname 'The Navigator'. He attempted it again, four years later, but died shipwrecked off the coast of Brazil.

In La Paz there is even a wind named after a privateer, or at least thought to be one. Watching the sunset that sets the bay ablaze in the late afternoon, the locals open their windows, stroll along the *malécon* (seafront) and breathe a sigh of relief. '*Por fin llega el coromuel!*' ('Finally the coromuel arrives!'), they all say. The coromuel starts blowing from the south-east in the evening, cooling the entire area and bringing welcome respite from the heat in the summer – it is normal for it to be 40 degrees in La Paz from June to September. Coromuel is probably a mispronunciation of 'Cromwell', though there is no consensus on the origins of the word. It was certainly the name of a ship, probably English, that appeared in the bay every evening at sunset, and according to some US historians, it appeared as early as the 17th century, sent by Cromwell himself to undermine Spanish dominance in the region. However, the story I was told by many people in La Paz seems more probable: that it all started in the 19th century. The brigantine would anchor in the middle of the bay, lower a longboat, and the sailors would row to one of the beaches that stretch from Pichilingue to Bahía Balandra, disembark and search for something or other. And so it carried on, every afternoon, in perfect timing with the wind, until the locals, at the time reduced to a small number and terrorised by the arrival of these foreigners, took to saying, '*Ya llegó el Coromuel!*' ('The Cromwell has arrived!'), mispronouncing the name on the stern. This went on for a month, then the *Cromwell* disappeared. A year later, again during the summer months, the *paceños* spotted the sail of the brigantine. There followed another month of regular evening visits, longboats at sea, disembarking on the beach, and so on. Exactly the same thing happened in the third year. According to the oral tradition handed down from those days, the *Cromwell*'s crew was looking for the loot of a galleon, the so-called *Nao de Manila*, which had been attacked and pillaged by English privateers, two of whom had been put in charge of burying it on a beach referred to, in the compulsory treasure map, as '*Ensenada de los Muertos*'. The captain of the *Cromwell* had the map but was missing a section. I kid you not .... During that third year of searching, one night a group of sailors mutinied and tried to kill the captain. It seems the latter slept with only one eye shut, because he reacted and fought back vigorously, giving the bosun time to rush over with the remaining loyal members of the crew. Once the mutineers were overpowered, the captain found the missing section of the map on their leader. The usual ritual ensued: longboats to sea, disembarkation. That was the last time the *paceños* saw the *Cromwell*. When a few days later some fishermen ventured to what is now called Ensenada de los Muertos, they discovered holes in the sand, and empty trunks that were corroded by sea salt, which looked very, very old. The treasure had been found. And the wind is still called 'Coromuel.'

Whether true or not, it is a beautiful story to tell your descendants.

There is a reason why La Paz swarms with treasure hunters, even though there is not a shred of evidence that they have ever found anything. The privateers used the bay, especially the cove in Pichilingue, nowadays the favourite mooring place of cruise ships, as a 'sanctuary.' Its name comes from Dutch privateers, headed by Van Spilbergen, that came from the port of Vlissinger. Through a series of repeated mispronunciations, the inhabitants of Baja California started calling those dreaded raiders *los pichilingues*. They would come and hide here to restock on drinking water and to escape Spanish warships. Baja was scarcely populated and almost without any important garrisons. We must also take an important fact into account: after pillaging a galleon, the privateers' ships were overloaded, which made them slow and hard to manoeuvre, so it is probable that the captains would choose to bury the trunks full of ingots and coins, meaning to go back for them when things had calmed down and the Spanish war fleet was not in pursuit. That is where the 'tradition' of maps originated – maps were jealously kept and often divided up in equal fragments amongst various officers, in order to render pointless any mutiny on the part of a section of the crew, or any plotting by those on board or in safe havens who hoped to lay their hands on the plunder. According to rumours flying about in La Paz, this area is swarming with buried treasure. I have even met someone who claims to be in possession of many secrets on that front.

Sergio Olachea Martínez is reputed to be the best masseur in La Paz and runs a vaguely New Age-type health centre: VIDA ALTERNATIVA. I do not doubt his ability to restore tense muscles and tired backs since the person who recommended that I talk to him speaks of him very highly. However, what attracts me to his cosy premises, scented with incense, is his in-depth knowledge of La Paz history. In fact, Sergio turns out to be a veritable goldmine of anecdotes and legends. I never imagined I would end up immersing myself in a dimension that is 'on the edges of reality.'

Sergio Olachea does not seem like someone out to convince you: he greets you in a blue coat and looks more like a confident doctor than a medium. However, he seems to trust me instinctively – or perhaps it is just the certainty of his convictions that makes him immune to the perplexity of sceptics. He tells me that with those people he feels it to be appropriate, on top of a massage, he uses hypnosis in order to take them back to their past lives. He believes in that and it does not occur to him that I might not. Either that or he just does not care. As far as he is concerned, I am a traveller introduced to him by a friend and he is not in the least bothered by what I think of him.

Among his many cases, he tells me of a man – he tells me his name, surname and even where he lives – who came to him for a massage about a year ago because of excruciating back pain in a localised area. However, even after many sessions, the relief was only momentary. In addition, he told Sergio that he had frequent nightmares that were real bloodbaths, in which he killed and disembowelled other men and was even himself stabbed in the ribs. This detail raised Sergio's suspicions, so he gave him a regression session (and this is where Sergio points out that these sessions are free of charge because his 'gift' cannot be translated into money; he charges for massages but not for hypnosis). So this man went back a few centuries and realised that he had been a privateer in a past life and that the cause of that stabbing pain was the sword that had run him through and killed him. He had, after all, cut throats, butchered, slashed and shot heaven knows how many Spaniards during his attacks on ships and the pillaging of their contents. The climax of the session came when he relived the moment immediately before his death in that distant and criminal lifetime, when he was burying a trunk full of doubloons and jewels on a neighbouring beach. At the end of the story, this man, who was a car mechanic, came to, thanked Sergio, and rushed to hire an excavator; he went to the precise point on that beach which he had seen whilst in the trance, and after a night of digging, he became the wealthy owner of an entire building – the one above the garage where he worked, in fact.

Sergio tells me many other stories like that, witnessed first hand or heard from others, and going back to the man who found the trunk, he expresses regret with angelic benevolence: 'He didn't even give me a gold coin as a souvenir. I don't expect payment, I repeat; just a bit of gratitude.' He then offers to take me to the recipient of the buried treasure – he says he would be glad to introduce me – though he explains immediately that he is an unhappy man. Even though the pain in his back and ribs disappeared that very day, he has suffered a string of misfortunes in his family, which only serve to prove that there is always a curse attached to the treasure of pirates or, in our case, privateers. I decline politely. I would not want the incarnation of the bloodthirsty murderer to lose his temper if I were to ask him where his current fortune comes from.

And these stories, too, are Mexico. We can be sceptical, and even laugh behind the storytellers' backs (though never to their faces, because Mexicans command respect – always), or act as though nothing has happened and go about our business. Yet one thing is certain: what we think of as absurd or surreal is considered totally normal for many people here. They neither judge, nor try and explain. It is just the way it is and that is that.

Finally, they keep saying that in La Paz, there are seven women for every man. It is an exaggeration but it is true to say that the female presence is overwhelming here compared to the number of men. Legend has it that this goes back to the times when Baja was the undisputed territory of Calafia's Amazons, who killed men after making love to them, and also any male babies. The historical truth is that the slaughter of rebellious Indios left behind only women and children until these people were totally wiped out. At the same time, the privateers, who were sometimes the founders of villages along the coast where they found safe havens, would take away their sons when they returned after a raid, most of whom met the obvious end for the adventurers of the time. In other words, they were killed during an attack. According to a particularly gruesome rumour, privateers used to kill their male children in order not to have future rivals, in keeping with their merciless lifestyle. The presence of so many privateers on the shores of the Sea of Cortez is illustrated by the existence of common surnames, such as Taylor, Fisher, Collins, Heart or Legs; all distant descendants of unlikely characters who buried treasure on neighbouring beaches.

In any case, at the start of the *malecón* there is an arch with the inscription: WELCOME TO LA PAZ, THE PORT OF ILLUSIONS.

3

Todos Santos

I GOT TO KNOW ALBERTO POLI, who sold music in one of Bologna's most famous record shops. I knew him to be a good bass player. We would chat about books and travel, he would help me obtain obscure CDs by Mexican bands, and he confirmed that in Italy, the works of Spaniard Joaquín Sabina – for whom I have developed a passion rather late in life – are unknown and impossible to buy, whereas in the rest of Europe – particularly Latin America – they are very famous and sold everywhere. One day, about five years ago, Alberto said, 'I've made up my mind: I'm going to live in Baja California. In Todos Santos.' It was the only important inhabited spot where I had never set foot. I had been to Baja California, the whole of it from north to south; and yet I had not yet been to Todos Santos.

So even though we stopped meeting up, we kept in touch. More or less once a month, Alberto would e-mail me a couple of photos. On top of being a bass player, musical expert and such a big fan of Bruce Springsteen that he could be his unauthorised biographer and hold the world record of attendance at his concerts, wherever they might take place, he is also a good photographer. So pictures with breathtaking colours would appear on my screen, with fiery dawns and sunsets, deserts and beaches that went on forever and faces of people against unique landscapes, the Pacific with its crashing waves, cacti and pelicans. I responded with friendly insults. Here am I, stuck in these interminable Po Valley winters, with fog and a dull drizzle that is not even heavy, proper rain, and grey everywhere, and you're making me feel even worse by sending me these photos. He always replied, on cue: so what are you waiting for? Come and see me. Meanwhile, I had been back to Mexico five or six times but always far from Baja. Eventually, in one e-mail after another, we concocted a plan to cover the whole peninsula, but in reverse, from the South to the North. He, with his trusted Canon around his neck, and I, with my Moleskine in my left hand and a pencil in my right, (in case it gets wet or damp, as graphite holds better than ink – as I have had occasion to find out). And so here we are, together – with my wife, Gloria – in Todos Santos.

We are on the Pacific, on the slope opposite La Paz, virtually on the Tropic of Cancer. The many gringos who stroll through or live here have probably never read Henry Miller's acclaimed novel, but they still seem to appreciate the essence of the Tropic. They do not rush around anymore, and some have even learnt a bit of Spanish. Surfers occupy the usual space between hippy and self-sufficient ascetic brotherhood. Many of them, together with Mexican painters and sculptors, are the life and soul of what is the highest concentration of art galleries on the entire peninsula. There are evenings when they all gather at the Hotel California, which has a patio with greenery and flowers, and where they improvise in noteworthy jam sessions. We often hear Bill Cherry, also known as 'the Blues Bible', who has hosted a legendary radio programme in Las Vegas for 25 years. Another one who hangs around here is Daniel Lanois, who co-produced, amongst others, some of Bob Dylan's historic albums, as well as some tracks by the Who and U2 – Bono also sneaks around these streets, where he could also come across Flea, of the Red Hot Chili Peppers. Lanois, also a musician, has recently composed a track called 'Todos Santos'. Peter Gabriel has also rented a house here, on the Pacific Coast, to draw inspiration from the sounds of the ocean which hurls itself against these shores with an almighty crash – a roar which, at night, provides the background to muffled thunderclaps that peak in thuds and make the ground vibrate – perhaps attracted by the reputation of this place and its microclimate that is so unusual in this torrid desert peninsula. The only people who claim never to have been here are the Eagles, which is extraordinary, considering that the Hotel California is now world famous thanks to their album of the same name. No one knows who started the rumour that it was this hotel that inspired them, but it is now too late to destroy the myth.

The true story of the Hotel California is peculiar; it was not built by a solitude-loving gringo but by an ambitious Chinese man. His surname was Wong and he became naturalised under the name of Ramón, having arrived here from Canton like so many other immigrants in 1947, after spending some time in Tabasco and therefore earning the nickname 'el Chino Tabasco.' Judging from the photos in the Todos Santos museum, Ramón Wong had the face of an alert and enterprising young man, with a roguish kind of charm, possibly handsome, and in any case, bold enough to court the daughter of a general of the *Revolución*. He settled in California with an impressive amount of land and various properties. The young woman fell for Wong's flattery and the general finally consented to the marriage. That was how the ambitious Wong built the first hotel in the area, in Todos Santos, which in 1947 was a dusty village that had sprung up around the oasis created by the stream that descends from the Sierra La Laguna, with the odd palm tree, and a lot of sand blown in by the Pacific breeze. Nowadays, the Hotel California is the main attraction in a town of 4,000 residents and a number of travellers. Few of its rooms are occupied on a permanent basis; it has a bar that serves special 'Hotel California' branded tequila, and a restaurant on the patio, where the food is good and there is music – lots of music – almost every night. An alternative for lovers of blues jam sessions is an Italian establishment, called Le Tre Galline (The Three Hens), a restaurant set up by Magda and Angelo, who came here from Salò in 2004. There are three hens painted on the door of the old house in Calle Topete – a spontaneous piece of work by Ezra Katz, a young artist who likes depicting scenes from everyday Todos Santos life – which is why they decided to give this name to their restaurant, where, besides good food, you can enjoy improvisations by passing musicians on the inner patio. It is here that Alberto and his group – The Barking Dogs – have played with the legendary Bill Cherry. Alas, it did not occur to anyone to record the evening. In any case, what the heck, it was 'improvised'.

On the endless beach of Todos Santos, which stretches dozens of kilometres to the north but is delimited in the south by the Punta Lobos promontory, I am greeted by a sight that leaves me speechless and ecstatic. The entire horizon is punctuated by the soft sprays of grey whales who approach the foreshore and disturb the sandy sea bed a few metres away from the shore. It is a crowd of enormous dark bodies covered in white concretions, in an expression of jubilation that looks like a game, imperturbable among the crashing waves which they dominate so effortlessly. Relaxed and majestic, agile and gigantic. Eventually, someone explains to me that they come all the way down here from far beyond the 'sanctuaries' further north where they go to mate and give birth, because the coast of Todos Santos is unique in Baja: a few metres from the shore, the coast drops down hundreds of metres, which prevents the whales beaching themselves, and allows them to come closer than they can anywhere else. As for their shifting tonnes of sand, some say it is in order to remove the parasites that torment them – the same parasites that form the stratum of lime on the keel of the boats, which grow weaker and come off more easily in the mild temperature of the waters at this latitude. Others say that they are in search of small molluscs that they filter through their baleens, but this second theory is less plausible since grey whales can go without food for up to six months, by consuming the fat reserves built up in the Arctic seas. The few people who arrive on the beach sit down and watch. We exchange satisfied glances and smiles. No one speaks, as though afraid to disturb an age-old ritual.

Before sunset, I walk towards Punta Lobos, which is half an hour's stroll on the sand, and go past a lagoon crowded with different kinds of birds, whilst geometrical formations of pelicans fly over the beach, often brushing the crests of the waves. Watching them, you are sure that they are doing it for fun – before they all converge in a small bay at the bottom, where fishermen are landing. Once there, among the lifeboats launched to gain more ground on the shore, I think of that poem by Baudelaire about the albatross: this 'king of the skies ... prince of the clouds accustomed to storms' who, once 'exiled to earth' becomes awkward and clumsy. 'He that was anon so handsome, is now ugly and comical when he must walk among humans.' The Pacific pelican is just like that: while flying, he swoops down air currents, moves gracefully just a few centimetres away from the water, caressing the crest of the waves like a skilled surfer, nose-dives straight for his prey and then resurfaces quickly. Meanwhile, I am surrounded by hundreds of staggering pelicans tripping over their large webbed feet, crowding one another while trying to keep their beaks, that seem to weigh a tonne, raised up. It is an absurdly long protrusion, which they use for catching the entrails of red snappers in mid-air. It has become a custom: the fishermen clean the fish on the beach, before selling them to the inhabitants of Todos Santos, who gather around the boats and throw the scraps to the pelicans, who over these many years have learnt not to fear humans. In fact, they have become so cheeky that every now and then a fisherman has to grab hold of a daring pelican's beak before he pinches a whole fish, and will throw him into the distance, forcing him to glide, and then toddle back, ready to gulp down several more kilos of succulent entrails. At one point, I witness some excitement: a pelican has managed to grab hold of a whole red snapper – a pink fish with fine meat – and is trying to swallow it. The fisherman grabs the pelican by the neck, stops him from ingesting, rams his hand down his beak and pulls out the fish, which he puts back into the box. Then he gives the large bird an affectionate slap, says, 'Don't do that again!' and threatens him with the nasty-looking knife he had temporarily put down in the boat. The seagulls also push in, and are even more aggressive since they swoop down from a height: a fisherman catches one mid-flight, spins him around by one of his wings and flings him out of the way. No one gets hurt, the humans have fun and the birds stuff themselves. Not far from here, the whales are circling around, doing somersaults and blowing breaths of spray.

The following morning, Alberto introduces me to an inhabitant of Todos Santos who represents the historical memory of the place. Nestor Agundez is the manager of the House of Culture, in which there is a little museum where you can hear about the arrival of Father Jaime Bravo, a missionary in the retinue of the Milanese Jesuit Salvaterra, who came to La Paz on foot in 1723 in order to found Todos Santos, where he discovered a freshwater spring able to provide for the hard life of a mission. Nestor is 83 years old, but looks 20 years younger; he lives in a brick house built in 1880, and gets very excited talking about the intense cultural activity of the town. It has at least two annual festivals. One is a Latin cinema festival where you can see excellent films that are regularly scrapped by international distributors, thus making Todos Santos into a kind of small, pioneering Sundance. The other one is an arts festival, in the loosest sense of the word, in that it includes 'popular' arts, such as folk dancing, and a programme full of theatrical events. While Nestor is talking, I look around. The living room walls are decorated with souvenirs, including photos of him when he was about 30 or younger. He looks like an idol from the golden age of Mexican cinema: pencil moustache, fine features, and a deep, proud gaze. He had his whole life ahead of him then, and Nestor Agundez must have grabbed it with both hands and built something lasting in Todos Santos, since I read, in a framed acknowledgement complete with the coat of arms of the Republic, TO ONE OF THE CREATORS OF BAJA CALIFORNIA, IN HONOUR OF HIS TIRELESS WORK AS TEACHER AND PROMOTER OF MEXICAN VALUES. When I ask him about the many foreign residents, he makes an ambiguous face and gives a vaguely diplomatic smile. 'Perhaps there are too many of them but as long as they treat us with respect, we also treat them with respect.' Then he adds, 'Of course, the North American community here is very active on the cultural front. Besides artists and galleries, they're also very keen to take part in organising the festivals and even financing them. However, the first couple of foreign artists to settle here were Spanish – Carlos and Marilù. They both paint and he is also a fine cabinet maker. In the end, they never left. They must be about 70 now and they also run a gallery.'

In Nestor's boundless and sharp memory, there is also ample room for the *Revolución*. That was before he was born but he tells me about *insurgente* Baja California's most fascinating character, even though this removed patch of land played only a marginal role in the decisive events of the time. This character was an extraordinary woman, Dionisia Viarino – known as 'La Coronela' – who was a midwife in Todos Santos. At this point, Nestor announces proudly, 'I, too, was born with Dionisia's help, in 1925!' Much earlier, Dionisia had distinguished herself by her courage during the bombing of Santa Rosalía when the federal gunboat *Querétaro* opened fire on the town as a reprisal for siding with Pancho Villa's revolutionaries. The midwife, who was young then, devoted herself to pulling out the injured from the rubble and eventually became Baja's Mata Hari. She sold tamales and tacos that she prepared herself, and would take a basketful to the federal troops, noting positions, pieces of artillery, the number of men and how many machine guns they had. Then, at nightfall, she would convey that information to Villa's supporters to help with their attacks. In the end, she was betrayed by a crooked politician who had switched sides and she was locked up in a jail in Guaymas, on the mainland. At the end of the war, once she was freed, Dionisia managed to track down the villain who had sold her out. It happened on a pier; she gave him a shove and pushed him right into the sea, screaming that she would not kill him because he was simply not worth the effort. She went back to being a *partera* (midwife) in Todos Santos, and was the first woman in the whole of Baja California to drive an automobile – which she needed to travel from one house to another, wherever there were children waiting to be born. So she ran along the sandy tracks of the 1920s, wearing goggles and a scarf, and was always covered in dust. Everybody now thinks of her as La Coronela, a rather military title, at odds with the photos Nestor showed me: Dionisia was beautiful, with delicate features and the expression of a dreamer – a charming idealist who put her ideals into practice with vigour but 'without ever losing her tenderness.'

BEFORE WE LEAVE TODOS SANTOS to start our long journey north, zig-zagging from one coastline to the other, we go to visit the ruins of the El Triunfo mines, which are dominated by a very tall chimney – the only building that has remained intact. The rest is nothing but crumbling bricks, rusty trolleys and machines. The trip is short and mostly along dirt roads, which is ideal for Alberto's powerful Bronco that seems to be made especially for climbing mountains and going on tracks that are part sand and part rock. At one point, we reach a fork Alberto does not remember ever having seen. We try to keep going along the old track, even though I have noticed a couple of rocks on the sides; in Mexico, they use them to block off a road that is interrupted, but these particular rocks have been moved. Because we have slowed down to avoid holes and subsidence, we are in time to see the chasm. The track disappears down a canyon. It is hard to tell whether it has been caused by a landslide, or whether they are building a bridge over it. In order to reverse, the Bronco clambers up the sides of the mountain, and when we drive past the rocks, we notice red and white ribbons in the dust. Until recently, the ravine before us was clearly cordoned off. I wonder who has removed the rocks and cordons and why. The alternative route is longer, but we finally arrive in the pueblo of El Triunfo.

There is even a cemetery, '*el Panteón Inglés*', with tombs like sarcophagi, but with no inscriptions or headstones. The relatives of English technicians and engineers working at the mine were probably buried here, even though the property belonged to the US El Progreso Mining Company. From 1878, they dug for gold and silver here, using large amounts of cyanide that polluted the precious layer of water in this desert territory, while the few trees were felled to build tunnel supports, and to keep fuelling the furnaces. The population of El Triunfo, which grew from 200 to 4,000, started staging protests against the destruction of the environment. For them, it was a paradox without solution because the mine kept everyone in work and allowed commerce and workshops to thrive; but on the other hand, they knew that without drinking water, trees, or the possibility of working on polluted land, the town was fated to die. The depletion of the gold seams put a drastic end to the matter. Nowadays, El Triunfo is a handful of little houses along the road; a parking spot for lorries, with a tiny church and an emporium where they sell just about everything. However, it is worth remembering that the El Progreso Mining Company was at least good enough not to impose its own company trade on miners and their families; unlike the powerful French mining company El Boleo, which forbade any independent commerce or craft in the areas it exploited. The commercial freedom that reigned in El Triunfo consequently encouraged the breeders in San Antonio, the tradesmen of La Paz and the farmers in Todos Santos, as during the time when mining was at its peak, at the turn of the century, thousands of people worked here and used the produce of the surrounding area.

4

The Friendly Gringos of Todos Santos

IN MEXICO, foreigners do not drink tap water, and they are right not to. It is not that there is a problem with the water itself, but rather that the system of water distribution includes large water reservoirs on rooftops, so as to have running water even during a drought, and it is difficult to keep such containers sterilised. Moreover, in Todos Santos, despite the perennial stream that comes down from the Sierra, water is a commodity more highly valued than elsewhere. The water would be perfectly drinkable, and taste good, too, if you could purify it without having to boil it. A few years ago, John and Jane returned from La Paz with a huge refrigerator at the back of their pick-up truck. This mammoth domestic appliance had an ingenious filtering system that allowed you to drink *agua de la llave* – tap water – and chilled water, at that! Friends took to going to visit John and Jane at all hours, for a glass of healthy, Antarctic-cold water. Jack would say, 'And to think what we've been missing all this time! This water is delicious!' To which Marion would add, 'You're the pioneers! Bruce and I are also going to go to La Paz soon to get an identical one.' As for Bob, he was ecstatic, 'I've cut down on iced beer since you've had this purified water!'

After about a year, there was a problem with the plug, which melted inside the socket because of an excessive electrical current. Panic time. A technician arrived a few days later. Once he had shifted the huge refrigerator with John and Jane's help, he commented innocently, 'Oh, look – you forgot to connect the filter pipe.'

So the water went straight from the tap to the refrigerator and was chilled but not purified by any filter.

The friendly colony of Todos Santos gringos who hung around John and Jane's house and who, up to then, had not experienced the slightest intestinal problem, suddenly panicked. The very next day, there were many cases of psychosomatic diarrhoea.

5

Espiritu Santo

OFF WE GO. We have a sturdy Dodge Durango for the long journey ahead. It is more spacious and more comfortable than the Bronco. The soundtrack is provided by Bruce Springsteen – Alberto is still hoping that the Boss will, sooner or later, drop in on Todos Santos. Stretches of cacti start to roll past us to the notes of Highway 29:

> In a little desert motel the air it was hot and clean
> I slept the sleep of the dead, I didn't dream
> I woke in the morning, washed my face in the sink
> We headed into the Sierra Madres 'cross the borderline
> The winter sun shot through the black trees
> I told myself it was something in her
> But as we drove I knew it was something in me
> Something that had been comin' for a long time
> And something that was here with me now
> On Highway 29

We go back to La Paz to take a motorboat that will take us to the island of Espiritu Santo, which is right in front of the bay, 20 kilometres long and 10 wide. Nobody lives there, but it is densely populated by animals – in particular by a colony of sea lions. You need about two hours to get there, and before passing the Canal de San Lorenzo in the Sea of Cortez, we go along Playa Balandra, one of the most beautiful beaches north of La Paz, where El Hongo stands, a volcanic rock sculpture shaped like a mushroom. The cap is so large and the stem so slight that you wonder why it does not crumble down into the sea. 'It did crumble down, actually,' the boatman tells me, 'But not because of high winds or rough seas. It was a bunch of idiots who tried to climb up it and snapped the narrow part of the stem.' The story of the restoration of this mushroom, immortalised in every postcard in the region, is touching. A married couple from the US used to holiday here every year. They were in love with Playa Balandra, where they had spent the happiest times of their lives. The woman then fell seriously ill, and before dying she asked her husband to scatter her ashes at sea, in front of El Hongo. In the meantime, the 'idiots' of unspecified nationality had caused it to collapse, so the husband requested permission from the government of La Paz to have it fixed at his own expense. And so it was, even though the delicate procedure of raising it out of the water and putting it back together so that it would last required special equipment and considerable effort. *Requiescat in pace*, anonymous lady.

Along the way, we brush past various small islands. La Gaviota stands out because of its volcanic origin; it is supposed to be black but looks almost entirely white because it is covered in the *guano* (bird droppings) of seagulls, which has given it its name. However, it is also frequented by the Pajaro Bobo, with their blue feet, and the Soula Nebouxii that thrilled Darwin in the Galapagos during his voyage around the world on board the barque *Beagle*. I wonder why Mexicans call this large sea bird – over 80 centimetres long – *bobo,* or 'idiot', or, at least, 'little fool.' Perhaps it is because its movements are somewhat comical as it totters on the ground on those striking, gaudy blue feet. However, when it flies it is an acrobatic diver and very agile underwater. Large frigate birds criss-cross above us – a species of huge swallow known here as *tijeras* (scissors) because of their forked tails. They do not seem so large from down here but when they come down to fish you can see that they have a wingspan of at least two metres. On another little island called El Merito, blue herons nest. Once we have admired them, the bow noses up and we zoom towards the ochre-coloured mass that is Espiritu Santo.

The boatman tells us about the gigantic pearl that is now prominently placed in the crown of the Queen of England, and which was fished out of the seabed right beneath the keel of our boat. Apparently, it was found during the first decade of the 20th century and according to popular imagination, which tends to increase its size with each new recollection, it is as large as a lemon, even though it is most probably about the size of a pigeon egg. Still, it is large enough to make many people yearn after it, including the British Consul, who spent years asking the governor to name a price, but all in vain; the pearl remained on display in the museum in La Paz. Finally, when the Consul admitted his intention to give it to the Queen, moved by an inexplicable monarchic largesse, Baja California gave it to the Crown of England, and received a visit from the Queen in thanks. Moreover, the fame of the world's largest pearl must have stimulated the imagination of John Steinbeck, who knew this area, and who wrote a brief but nonetheless intense novel – strangely imbibed with Mexican spirit – called *The Pearl*. In it, he tells the story of Kino, a fisherman who must go through many ordeals after his dream of escaping misery has apparently come true, as his life is slowly capsized by Fortune's fickle hand. It is no coincidence that Steinbeck called his protagonist Kino – but that is a name I will come back to later.

In Mexico, I have learnt not to be surprised when I come across coach drivers who turn out to have an in-depth knowledge of their country's history; tyre merchants and mechanics often know more than many anthropologists; dancers in Aztec costumes can turn out to be repositories of vanished civilisations and many boatmen know all there is to know not only about the secrets of the sea but also about

Prehistoric migrations. As we go along Punta Bonanza, with its chalky red-streaked rock which sometimes assumes the shape of grand castles sculpted by the wind, our bosun tells us that in the caves of Isla Espiritu Santo, they have recovered heaps of oysters – leftovers from early inhabitants' lunches and dinners – which, when tested for Carbon-14, revealed a surprising fact: that they date back to an era before the Mongolian migrations from the Bering Strait, which gradually populated the Americas. This means that the ancestors of the Perico Indios were already here. They left a few rock paintings in a cave near Playa de la Ballena.

We come across various kayaks and very occasionally a sailing boat. A yachtsman created something we now call 'the Candelarios Library' here – it is a cavity in a cliff, where he got into the habit of leaving books he had read. The news spread and for years now, this hole, easily reachable even by those with no talent for climbing, has become a swapping centre for second-hand books.

At one point, we think we see a couple of dolphins, but the boatman's trained eye corrects us: those are not the dorsal fins of cetaceans but the fins of a giant ray, sunbathing. We come closer. It looks sumptuous, to say the least; its black rhomboid wings are about eight metres wide and it must weigh a couple of tonnes. Even if it only feeds on plankton, it must be quite a shock to come across it while out for a swim, especially since it is an animal that is very inquisitive towards divers. It is playful and surely very intelligent, given the development of its brain and in particular of its telencephalon – the part of the brain which in humans corresponds to the most developed functions, and all of the voluntary actions in the body.

Baja's giant rays tend to do spectacular leaps. The females even give birth like that, flying out of the water. This ray just ignores us, and then plunges with the elegance of a ghost of the abyss, leaving behind a whirlpool. The reason it takes acrobatic leaps has engendered a series of hypotheses, the most obvious being that it is a mating ritual, the most practical, that it gets rid of parasites and remora that cling to the rays' skin with their irritating suckers. However, I would rather believe biologist David Sloan Wilson, who is certain that rays jump to express joy. He says that it is a game, and asserts that many forms of play have an evolutionary value, in that they strengthen social interaction within a species.

Espiritu Santo is actually made up of two islands, since there is a canal on the northern tip which separates Isla Partida from its older sister, and further north there are Los Islotes – tiny islands populated by hundreds of sea lions. They look like seals but our boatman ticks us off: seals are much smaller, and indeed their jaws, fangs and roars immediately confirm that they are sea lions. Actually, the stout males raise their voices to impress their harem, while the young ones dive into the water to play with some strange creatures with coloured bulges on their backs – a group of German day-trippers in wetsuits, flippers and masks (the water is icy in February) are swimming and shrieking with wonder through their mouth-pieces, while the crowd of sea lions surrounds them, often stopping to investigate them with curiosity. Only one thing jars in this idyllic scene of paradise lost and regained: a powerful stench of dung. You would think you were in a pigsty somewhere south of Modena. Well, there is not an unoccupied rock and those playful and noisy pachyderms crowd every corner as they love idling around in the sun, so between the sweat and the dung they are constantly producing....

We keep circumnavigating, along a good 50 kilometres of coastline, sliding through shadowy arches and past walls of pinkish rock where fish eagles nest. After pausing on a beach that could rival the holiday resorts of the Caribbean, towards the end of the day we go past Bahìa San Gabriel. Near the coast, you can still see the remains of a colony of French settlers who came all the way here in the 18th century. Their dream was to cultivate pearl oysters, so they set up a farm and built houses and city walls, but in the end had to capitulate to nature, which on Isla Espiritu Santo seems welcoming and benevolent to all creatures except humans. The sea and the wind have wiped out any attempt to bequeath to posterity the vestiges of a past that is now long gone.

We return to the harbour, going past the large peninsula of El Mogote. For many years it was strictly forbidden to build here, but now you can see cranes and the skeletal structures of scaffolding. Those ever-multiplying spreaders of cement have managed to obtain something, after all. The Coromuel cools the air and La Paz looks splendid, seen from the sea at sunset. There is a seafood feast waiting for us at the Bismarck. I do not dare ask the crafty managers why on earth they have called it that: it is a popular restaurant in the most literal sense of the word. The food is simple, and therefore excellent, and a huge oil painting of the battleship *Bismarck* dominates the wall, sailing through the leaden waters of the North Sea, with its powerful guns and its starboard hull streaked in different shades of grey. This camouflage failed to save it from the British torpedoes that hit its rudder after the Royal Navy had been riled by the sinking of HMS *Hood* – the pride and joy of the British Navy – and the driving-off of HMS *Prince of Wales*, in a two-against-one battle that had humiliated His Majesty and infuriated Churchill. But what does the *Bismarck* have to do with a *mariscos* (seafood) restaurant on the *malecón* (seafront) of La Paz, in Baja California Sur? Nothing at all, but so what? Halfway through dinner, a group of mariachis come in – the craziest I have ever heard in Mexico. They remind me of the Brutos of my Italian childhood. They are tone deaf, and one of them pulls the most outrageous faces and every so often makes animal noises. The irresistible, semi-involuntary comedy of the trio makes everyone laugh. The waiters roll their eyes. On the wall, the *Bismarck* sails on, unperturbed, towards its cruel fate. Meanwhile, on the *malecón*, they are rehearsing for the carnival with a group of graceful teenage girls who are dancing, all ethereal. *Estamos en México.*

There is a place in central La Paz that should not be missed. It is the Hotel Yeneka, the haunt of famous musicians in search of anonymity, and of penniless travellers. It is a sort of museum of bits and pieces. The patio, full of greenery and flowers, is cluttered with rusty vintage cars, unusable type-writers and sewing machines, cow horns, stuffed animals, huge pieces of machinery and colourful shells, as well as a large collection of sombreros hanging from the ceiling in the hall where the wide-open French windows display the prominent sign: FREE MARIJUANA. All the rooms – only 20 in total – are fairly Spartan, albeit comfortable, and have fres-coes on the wall behind the bed, with lunar landscapes and deserts – absurd and surreal. Yeneka is a Perico word meaning sun-dried deer meat. The owner is Doctor Miguel Macías, a medical doctor; he inherited the hotel from his father, who had it built 60 years ago. On the cluttered business card you read, 'The home of the friends of the world, a space for reflection, a museum for the recycling of ideas.' Rates can be negotiated, depending on how long you are staying, since at the Hotel Yeneka there are the usual travellers, but also those who plan on staying one night and end up staying a year. It must be the easy-going atmosphere of La Paz.

6

Endless Cacti

W E RESUME OUR JOURNEY at dawn, after filling up with petrol – a must when you find a petrol station in Baja, as we will not come across many more from here on. The Federal Mexico 1 from La Paz goes west, into the heart of the peninsula, before veering north towards Ciudad Constitución, which we are aiming to reach before nightfall. The band of asphalt unrolls through an endless plain of cacti, and in the background there is the Mesa del Cerro Colorado. Our soundtrack is Neil Young's *Unknown Legend*, which tells the story of a girl riding a Harley Davidson along a desert road. There is heavy traffic: we only come across another vehicle roughly every quarter of an hour. Sometimes it is a Harley, one of them surely driven by a girl. There are even reckless cyclists who will have to find some shade within the hour, before the ruthless midday sun starts pounding down. For now, it is cool. In the winter, the temperature range is wide. At night, we need a blankets even in La Paz, which is known for having sweltering heat six months a year. However, as we penetrate the desert, the temperature rises during the day. It never reaches the 45 or 50 degrees you would get in the summer, but the dry climate makes the 25, or at most, 30 degrees that await us perfectly pleasant. In other words, crossing Baja in February is heavenly. It is in this captivating desolation that the variegated family of Cactaceae appeared dozens of millions of years ago, gradually spreading to Canada and Patagonia. Of the 120 Baja varieties, at least 80 are native and cannot be found even in the neighbouring Sonora desert, on the shore opposite the Sea of Cortez. Their secret is their slowness. From the small barrel cactus to the robust *saguaro* (American cactus) and 20-metre tall cereus, from the tiny buttons, half-hidden in the dusty sand, to the monumental plants that stand out on the plains – all grow slowly and often live for over a century, sometimes even two – as in the case of the majestic cereus.

Over thousands of years, they have turned their leaves into claws, and birds in search of water are often harpooned to death. To withstand the 50 degrees of heat in the direct sunlight, they have reduced their external surface as much as possible by transferring the process of photosynthesis to within their trunks. Some can weigh up to ten tonnes and are actual water cisterns, with a capacity of 3,000 litres. It rains very seldom – sometimes there is no rain for as long as five years in a row – but when there is a downpour, the cacti do not miss a single drop. Even a few minutes after the shower, the desert is completely dry. The long, ramified roots absorb all the moisture and store it in the spongy tissue, holding onto it by way of the stomas hidden in the cavities beneath the surface of the trunk. Thus, they can still breathe, but the loss of vapour is reduced by 40 per cent, since the waterproof substance that coats them prevents perspiration. There are other, smaller cacti that live just beneath the sand and let their outer parts dry up. Then as soon as there is a splash of rain, even after a decade, a bunch of tiny leaves, or even a pulpy flower, bursts forth. Life here is a constant, silent waiting game.

There is no shortage of trees, even if these now look like cacti. The Idria Columnaris is another species native to Baja. It is more widely known as the Cirio and is also called Boojum because of a highly imaginative botanist who loved Lewis Carroll's *The Hunting of the Snark*, in which it is the name of strange desert inhabitants. It is an odd-looking creature, like a sort of giant carrot, and someone once called it 'the court jester' of the reigning cacti. In effect, it is a trunk that takes on the most extraordinary shapes, arching its back until it forms circles beneath the sky or large question marks in the desert, with bunches of tiny leaves on the top – the only proof of life in a body that is naked for most of the year, except for when it sprouts a plume of yellow flowers that reaches 18 metres in height. The same applies to the Baja Elephant Tree, *Pachycormus discolor*, which has a trunk that is one and a half metres in diameter and which is covered in tiny leaves after a single downpour; a botanist once described it as 'splendid and grotesque.' It barely reaches six metres in height, but stretches its twisted branches across a 12-metre diameter. It stays dormant for months or even years, looking dead – but all it takes is the gift of a water-yielding cloud in the sky, and within a day it is covered in red and pink buds which can blossom over several weeks, to spectacular effect.

The yucca is another predominant plant in the peninsula's vegetation. Robust and belonging to the lily family, it likes areas with frequent fog – this morning, a milky-white blanket reveals landscapes of bewitching beauty – and feeds via the winds that blow in from the ocean, carrying precious moisture. The yucca lives in symbiosis with a tiny white Lepidoptera, without whose help it could not reproduce: the little butterflies fly at night, gather pollen from spring flowers, roll it into balls together with their own eggs, and deposit the balls on other flowers, fertilising them. And even if half the seeds are eaten by the larvae that come out, the other half go on to create new yuccas. Without that particular butterfly, the yucca would be extinct.

This has been an *año felíz* (a fortunate year) for Mother Nature in Baja: it rained several times a few days ago and on the sides of the roads we admire incredible patches of little flowers that are normally not seen for decades at a time. Around us, as far as the eye can see, cereuses abound, and seem to form an impenetrable forest, even though, in reality, they grow far apart from one another. Their vast numbers create the effect of a barrier that goes on forever. A few months from now, if this springtime manages to take advantage of the precious recent moisture, the white flowers that will blossom on the tops of the cacti and which give out a powerful scent during the night will yield a golden, thorny fruit which used to be much appreciated by the Indios; when they were still living here they would extract and roast the seeds. Then as now, however, the cereus offers above all a very sturdy trunk, which holds up the pillar of green flesh. It is a skeleton pierced by vaguely geometric patterns, tough as steel, yet flexible and immune to parasites, and often used for making beams, fences and roof supports. I have seen them all over Mexico, but here they are part of the popular architecture – bearing in mind that there is little left that is 'popular' in depopulated Baja.

The road is straight, and vanishes beyond the horizon in a succession of quivering and evanescent waves rising from the heat of the asphalt, as though it were immersed in water; it does not actually have any curves for hours on end. It is easy to let yourself slip into cinematic imagination: this is the desert road par excellence. Tow trucks as long as trains make it easy for us to overtake them by using their indicator. In Mexico, they do it the other way around. If the left indicator light flashes, then you can go. We are greeted by horns, since we are among the very few travellers along the México 1. You can trust Mexican *traileros*; just wait for them to tell you what to do. I take it in turns with Alberto to drive the Dodge Durango. In Italy, it is a crime against humanity to use this 5,000 cc double-traction engine in a historical centre, but here it is considered perfectly normal. The gears are automatic and slow, as is appropriate for a long-distance vehicle that must last rather than get there in a rush. Because what is important, between leaving and arriving, is the actual journey, you find yourself focusing on what you see on the way, rather than on your actual destination. For example, you come across 'refreshment points' that are little huts built of unbaked bricks and a sheet metal roof, with a family sitting around the drinks fridge, where you can have something cooked on a red-hot plate heated by gas from a rusty cylinder. The laundry is hanging out to dry, maybe there is even a mule, or moulting hens – perhaps even a pig, for those who crave more comfort; but you never find misery. Misery seems to have been eradicated from Baja. There is dignified poverty, and silence interrupted by the honking of a gigantic, 12-axle Kenworth Ken-Mex slowing gears, so that even children stop shouting, puzzled by our presence. The bravest asks, 'Where do you come from?'

'Ooh ... A long way away ... From Italy – do you know where that is?'

The boy shakes his head.

'It's in Europe. On the other side of the Atlantic.'

'And how long does it take to get here?'

'Twenty hours by plane.'

He thinks, does some mental arithmetic, considers how you can stay up on a plane for 20 hours, then asks, 'Yes, but ... How long is it by car?' How do you explain that you cannot get here by car all the way from Europe?

Here, if you ask about distances, no one speaks in kilometres but in hours' drive. We keep an eye on the map. We know there is a particular signpost, then a diversion. Here it is: El Imposible. I do not know what exactly is 'impossible' among this cluster of huts on the edge of the asphalt, surrounded by desert – perhaps any possibility of tourist development. Finally we take a right turn onto a sandy track that will take us to the first Jesuit mission of our journey.

After an hour of driving, leaving dust clouds in our wake, clear skies begin to appear in our windscreen, and the peaks of the Sierra La Giganta ahead, and the panorama suddenly unfolds onto a huge flat plateau: a yellow ochre church, a long, semi-abandoned cottage, a dilapidated little house, a cow that stares at us in astonishment and a man with a sombrero, who greets us while watering a vegetable garden. We are at the San Luis Gonzaga Chiriyaquí mission, founded in 1737 by the Jesuit Lambert Hostell. Father Juan Jacobo Baegert later had the church built, but in the meantime, whilst breaking his back trying to cultivate land that is *imposible* to farm (the sign now makes sense), he wrote a text that was fundamental for an understanding of places that used to be beyond our world: *Noticias de la península Americana de California*. ('News from the American Peninsula of California'). The sun is blinding – a yellowish whiteness that dominates the view. The mission is 'inhabited', in that there are a few families living here, cultivating the small amount of land with the scarce water supply. They explain that the large cottage is going to be done up and fitted with solar panels to provide electricity. For now, they occupy only a small part of it, while next to the church – well maintained, with a secluded cemetery at the back – stands another abandoned building, with airy arches but no roof. In the 18th century, about 500 Indios of various ethnicities lived in the mission, and the bell up there is still the one put up by Father Baegert, even though there is no longer a priest to say mass and only on special occasions does one come from the nearest town. Recently, the image of Saint Luigi Gonzaga has returned to the little church, having been found in La Paz after going 'missing' in 1914 owing to some mishap or other. The mission was probably sacked during those years of revolutions and counter-revolutions.

Separately, we both spend at least an hour meandering around this space, untouched by time, enjoying the sense of alienation and of rarefied spirituality that still permeates the place.

7

The Jesuits of Baja

WHEN I FIRST ARRIVED IN MEXICO, in 1982, I happened to try one of the most common restaurant wines, at least among the restaurants that actually serve wine. It was called 'Padre Kino' and came in a peculiar bottle. It was a litre container with a wide mouth and a narrow neck, of the type used as a unit measure in old Italian taverns. Consequently, the cork was actually a jam jar lid. I tried it once, only never to drink it again; deciding there and then that the countless brands of Mexican *cerveza* were not only more appealing than the wine, but were in no way inferior to some of the best European beers, thanks to the tradition of German beer manufacturers emigrating to Mexico as early as the time of Porfirio Díaz, and also to the skill of the Mexican beer manufacturers, who succeeded in creating varieties that are now exported worldwide.

Red and white Padre Kino continues to be sold in supermarkets: it has the same dubious quality of our pseudo-wine in cartons. I would have spent years trying to work out why it was called by that name. Still, the 'Padre' on the yellow label did not surprise me, since one of the carbonated water brands I used to drink in the Eighties was called Agua de Lourdes and came complete with a little Madonna on the bottle. Yet there were no miracles involved, and once again, I decided it was better to go for the *cerveza*.

Eusebio Francesco Chini was born on 10 August 1645 in Segno, a district of Taio, in Val di Non, then the Episcopal Principality of Trento. After completing his studies in the Jesuit College in Trento and distinguishing himself in Natural Sciences, he took the vows of the Society of Jesus and in 1681 went to Mexico, then called Nueva España, as a missionary. A tireless explorer on horseback (they estimate that Father Chini's expeditions covered an area of at least 130 square kilometres), he was responsible for the early geographical maps of Baja California, and that is how Baja California officially became recognised as a peninsula, and not – as the Spaniards believed – an island. A firm defender of the natives' rights, he lived among ethnic Pimas in the North West, and entered into open conflict with the Church hierarchy about colonialism. He fought wholeheartedly his entire life against the use of Indios as slave labour in the silver mines, and as exportable labourers to suit the needs of landowners. He became known to everyone as Father Kino (the Italian 'k' sound in 'Chini' sounded like 'Tchini' in Spanish, and was then mangled into 'Chino', which means 'Chinese' until, finally, a 'k' was adopted to harden the consonant), and devoted himself to the development of that arid land, where he taught the Indios about livestock and agriculture. The fact that he encouraged vine cultivation probably inspired the producers of the wine that bears his name, even though there are producers in Baja California that offer far better quality wine.

In the states of north-western Mexico, Sonora and Baja California in particular, there are countless streets and squares named after Father Kino – and even two cities: Bahía Kino and Magdalena de Kino, where he died in 1711. Even in Arizona, Father Kino is considered a benefactor worth remembering. On the occasion of the tricentenary of his arrival to those desert areas – now large border territories between Mexico and the United States – sculptor Julián Martínez forged three identical statues that represent him on horseback. One of them stands at the entrance to the motorway that links Magdalena to Hermosillo, the second one is on Kino Parkway, in Tucson, and the third is in Val di Non, where Father Kino began his adventurous life. When, in 1991, they moved it to Segno after a long journey from Sonora, diplomats representing both Mexico and the United States took part in the ceremony, as a tribute to the meritorious Jesuit missionary.

Even though he produced the first maps of what he refers to in his writings as '*Mi querida California*' ('My beloved California'), Father Kino was never able to settle in Baja California and establish his mission because of an explicit prohibition from the Church, who, besides favouring Franciscans (who were more submissive to the desires of colonialism than Jesuits) also feared that his absence from Sonora would reignite the revolt of the far from tamed natives of the north-west.

However, Father Kino succeeded in helping Jesuit missions get underway in Baja. The first people he persuaded to relocate to that strip of inhospitable and inaccessible desert in the midst of the sea were two fellow Italians: Father Juan María Salvatierra – the hispanicised name of Milanese Giovanni Maria Salvaterra – and Francesco Maria Piccolo from Palermo. Having obtained permission from the Father Provincial of the Society of Jesus in Mexico City – who warned them that absolutely no funds would be obtained from the Crown, and that they would have to rely on their own means – the two men eventually ventured onto a *galeota* (slave galley) that travelled from the coast of Sinaloa and crossed the Sea of Cortez. In vain, they had hoped until the very last that Father Kino would be able to sail with them. However, the explorer and missionary had devoted himself to raising funds through collections, and, incurable dreamer that he was, he had even had a ship with two masts built in the middle of the desert in the Caborca mission, located over 100 kilometres from the coast. In the end, there was no way of transporting or launching it, so the two missionaries had to spend part of their own meagre funds to pay for their transport. Father Kino's idea had been to provide the Jesuits with their own ship so they would be independent and not get stranded in the middle of nowhere, but he did not realise just how impossible it would be for mules to drag a heavy galley with masts across the desert.

Kino, Salvaterra and Piccolo had agreed that their enterprise would be entirely peaceful and that any platoons of soldiers that would eventually escort missions would come under the orders of the Jesuits and not the Crown where any local decision was concerned. Even the law would be administered by the missionaries so that the soldiers would not be able to apply tough sentences in cases of crimes or revolts. And so began the Utopia of Baja California's Jesuits, full of insurmountable obstacles owing to the ruthless natural conditions that awaited them, and to all kinds of adversity, and compounded by their own self-denial, naivety and miscalculations that would sentence their project to inevitable failure.

Salvaterra and Piccolo disembarked on 12 October 1697 in a spot about 200 kilometres north of the bay of La Paz. Fifteen years earlier, the first missionary settlement, San Bruno, had been created there, but it was later abandoned because it was impossible to cultivate the surrounding land. The two Jesuits travelled south on foot until they reached Ensenada de San Dionisio: a bay protected by Carmen Island and full of greenery thanks to the freshwater springs nearby. That was where they founded the first mission, Nuestra Señora de Loreto, in memory of their faraway Italian birthplace, and of the sanctuary of the same name in the Marche region. Very soon, Loreto became the colonial stronghold in Baja, and took on the title of Real, or 'land belonging to the king'. It was no longer merely an evangelising mission, but was populated by so many settlers that it became the capital of the Californias. Meanwhile, the Jesuits had brought with them olive trees, grapevines, lemons, oranges, figs, date palms and all sorts of seeds. Their dream was to develop agriculture among the Indios, to help save them from the expansionist Spanish Crown that treated them like slaves in the rest of Mexico. In 1699, Father Piccolo moved further north and founded the second mission, San Francisco Javier. Moreover, the arrival of other missionaries sent over by the tireless Father Kino allowed the work to continue: another mission was founded in 1705 in the oasis of Mulegé, and called Santa Rosalía in honour of the saint from Palermo. Then came San José de Comondú, and many others, in little more than half a century, until there were 17 of them scattered between San José del Cabo in the far south and Santa María de los Ángeles in the north.

Relations with the Indios were based on teaching: in general, missions were set up near geographically semi-sendentary communities which the Jesuits would try and involve in working the fields and developing crafts, persuading them to give up their nomadic lifestyle. The few escort soldiers there were did not form proper garrisons and had to obey the missionaries; any abuse was punished severely and mistreatment of the indigenous population was rare. This encouraged closeness and mutual respect. Within a few decades, a village had grown up around each mission, and the Indios worked the land and raised livestock. They had accepted the new religion only in part, but in general the process of evangelisation was going well, even though it involved the gradual crumbling of traditions, including the Indios' knowledge of medicinal plants and of the equilibrium of the wild and harsh natural conditions. Admittedly, the Jesuits were eager to learn about these aspects of Indio culture, although they also tried hard to impose chastity and marital bonds, monogamy, and a concept of authority which included rules and punishment. The Jesuits tended to delegate the government of the village to the Indios themselves and soon *temastianes* appeared – 'those who teach others', or teachers – Indios who had become experts at agriculture or crafts, and who in turn encouraged the spread of these skills. Food shortages and occasional famine when drought destroyed the crop were always the Jesuit missions' principal enemies. However, there were two far more destructive hidden dangers that would cause the demise of Baja California's Utopia: disease, and the greed of the new landowners.

As the port of La Paz developed, sailors started arriving, and as Loreto grew in size contingents of soldiers would alternate. From sneaky influenza to the lethal smallpox virus and syphilis, along with typhus, dysentery and malaria, illness decimated the Indios, who lacked immunity against these unknown diseases. The fact that the population was all gathered around missions helped to spread contagion at a deadly rate. The three ethnic groups present in Baja when the Spaniards arrived – the Perico in the South, the Guaycura in the area between La Paz and Loreto and the Cochimi in the central North – also represented three distinct language groups. At the beginning of the 17th century, they were estimated at about 50,000. Half a century later, there were only 200 Perico remaining, almost all afflicted with various diseases. In 1762, the indigenous population of Baja barely reached 10,000, and it continued to decrease until at the beginning of the 19th century there were only 3,000 Indios remaining, living in the far north, in the Río Colorado area. They had only survived because of their total isolation and therefore lack of contact with 'civilisation'. Unlike certain species of animals or plants, there is no precise date for the 'extinction' of the Guaycura, the Perico and the Cochimi, but they have not been around since then. Nowadays, the only Baja inhabitants with Indio traits are descendants of the Yaqui and the Mayo, who migrated here in the 1800s to work in the mines and build cities and roads.

Many revolts were stamped out with bloodshed. There were various cases of indigenous communities rebelling after noticing that evangelisation was putting an end to everything that represented their identity as a people. So more as an instinctive reaction than a calculated decision, as disease and humiliation degenerated into a growing number of deaths, they took up their bows and arrows. The same Jesuits who left us texts and records all agree that Californian natives had an open and cordial attitude, that they were peace-loving, that they devoted themselves to hunting and picking forest fruits and were alien to tribal wars. If you treated them with respect, they respected you in return. However, they were not 'meek' beasts of burden, and in many cases the Jesuits did not manage to keep in check rough soldiers and greedy and violent new settlers whose abuse was bound to lead to tragedy. The first widespread rebellion broke out in 1734 in the Santiago mission, south of La Paz, and the missionary Lorenzo Carranco was killed in the fray. It then spread to San José del Cabo. Here too, the Jesuit in charge of the mission, Nicolás Tamaral, was killed by Indio arrows and his body was burned. The rebels destroyed buildings and threw crosses and bells into the flames. The same fate awaited the nearby mission of Santa Rosa de Todos Santos, but in this case, Father Sigismundo Taraval, originally from Lodi, managed to flee in the nick of time. Reinforcements arrived from the Sinaloa coast to the Loreto garrison which, under the command of Captain Esteban Rodríguez Lorenzo, marched south to stamp out the revolt. However, the Indios did not want to fight: theirs was not a 'revolution'. They had just risen through an instinctive and rather belated hope for survival. They would hide and not attack the soldiers even when the latter were within shooting range of their bows. Meanwhile, the troops captured women and children, making no distinction between the families of the 'rebels' or the 'peaceful', and deported them far away from that area. With only men remaining, even the peaceful villages were sentenced to extinction. The military hanged a number of rebel 'chiefs', and any pleading on the part of the Jesuits that they stop the reprisals and, instead, exercise Christian forgiveness, was fruitless. The last Perico revolt in the south took place in 1740, and was stamped out even more harshly and indiscriminately. A few years later, an ethnic minority of Guaycura-speaking Huchiti attempted an uprising, but within a few days the soldiers ensured that their small number were totally wiped out.

Another inescapable pitfall for the Jesuits' Utopia was so-called 'progress'. In Baja, there were copper deposits, and to a lesser extent precious metals and even cobalt. The Real Erario da Madrid requested that these treasures be mined, and it was not long before mining experts began to arrive. They needed a workforce and a lot of timber to build the mining galleries. A human and natural disaster was in the making. In addition, there were the pearls in the bay of La Paz, and the strongest among the Indios were able to hold their breath longer than the Spaniards and dive deeper. The Jesuits fought bravely against mining and pearl fishing, trying to demonise both, but in vain: the Spanish monarchs put increasing pressure on the Church hierarchy to get rid of these 'obstacles' to progress, namely the missionaries from the Society of Jesus, who were stubbornly against any exploitation of the Indios. They believed the Indios should cultivate fields and produce oil, dates, citrus fruit and even wine, in the name of a benevolent and merciful God.

On 2 April of the year of our Lord 1767, King Charles III of Spain issued a decree expelling Jesuits from all American territories. The vague explanation given was 'reasons of State'. However, that was a dream come true for many mine owners, pearl-fishing companies, livestock breeders and big landowners in general. This was the King's way of 'modernising' neo-Hispanic society and the imperial economy, whereas the Jesuits represented a dangerous attachment to the past, to a farming world of poverty and respect for equilibrium, where only what was necessary to the community was produced with nothing for commerce or profit: a Utopia that had become intolerable and unacceptable.

In Roland Joffé's unforgettable film *The Mission*, we see

how in the Paraguay missions, during the tragic year of 1767, some Jesuits staged a resistance against the colonial army. The ex-mercenary, played by Robert De Niro, takes up arms to fight alongside the natives, while the character played by Jeremy Irons chooses sacrifice in order to convey his message of peace by not answering violence with violence. The Jesuits of Baja California acted like the latter, and left with sadness and in silence, hoping that their attitude would spare the lives of the indigenous communities. They could not imagine that the Indios would be wiped out within just a few decades.

A contingent under the command of Captain Gaspar de Portolá – responsible for deporting all the Baja Jesuits – sailed from the port of San Blas (nowadays in the state of Nayarit). It landed at San José del Cabo and on 24 December, Christmas Eve, reached Loreto. There it gathered all the Jesuits from the peninsula's missions. Some had lived and worked there for at least 30 years. Father Benno Ducrue is said to have written in his memoirs, 'Only a mother whose child dies feels the pain I feel in abandoning the Indios of our missions.' Captain Portolá organised boarding at night to avoid the risk of a hostile crowd gathering: a useless precaution, since the Jesuits walked down the beach through a double row of Indios and mixed-race servants who knelt and wept softly as they passed: a farewell ceremony so heartbreaking that according to Father Ducrue's memoirs, even the captain of the King's soldiers could not hide his emotion.

8

Towards Puerto San Carlos

WE GO AGAIN along the track from the San Luis Gonzaga Chiriyaquí Mission to the Federal 1, to get to Ciudad Constitucíon, which we will use as a base to get to Puerto San Carlos, on Bahía Magdalena.

Ciudad Constitucíon is a junction between inland territory and the Pacific, a crossing point for lorry drivers and a place where the goods of the area converge; a large, dusty village made of low houses. It does not have a proper town centre but has sprawled beside the motorway that runs along Baja Sur. The hotel where we spend the night is from the Mexico I recognise after years of roaming, the Mexico that looks as though it will never change or, at least, will grant me the biological time never to see it change, and I find that thought comforting. Desolate and welcoming at the same time, with no pretence of trying to attract tourists; simple, functional and roomy, with a lady in reception who makes me wait a good 15 minutes while she chats on the telephone with some relative or other. When she finally hangs up, she bursts out laughing and motions the receiver as if to say, 'You know what it's like when you have a large family.' Outside, in the side streets, there are plenty of *taquerías* (taco bars) for travellers: we eat the best tacos since leaving La Paz, strictly *al pastor* (marinated): pork *carnitas* (braised) with onion, *cilantro* (coriander) and spicy sauces – delicious. The music belts out from the stereo, *rancheras* ballads, occasionally drowned out by the thundering exhaust pipe of a passing lorry. A stray dog fixes its imploring eyes on my tortilla. The Pacifico beer is ice-cold and I would not trade it for the best wine in the world. The woman behind the stall, who is casually fussing over the red-hot plates, her quick movements adeptly turning over the meat and vegetables and cooking them perfectly, looks with surprise at the green chili I put in my tacos, perhaps expecting me to choke because it is too spicy. When I do not, she is curious and asks me where the hell I come from, then says something like, 'Oh, I thought you couldn't be a gringo.' I feel really at home.

At night, we are so tired, we sleep soundly. Even the local lads celebrating something or other by turning up the volume of their car stereos to the full cannot disturb us. Early in the morning, we take the left turning beneath the large sign that says PUERTO SAN CARLOS. It is the *carretera* (highway) number 22, nice and straight, and lined with lampposts, on top of which fish eagles have built their nests. In Puerto San Carlo, we are welcomed by the reek of boiled sardines that permeates the air. It comes from the large tinned fish factory. The whole local economy revolves around fishing, which supplies the factory. We drive along sandy streets, among grey brick houses. At one point, something that looks like a 'main road' crosses an open space where a highly-animated football match is taking place. The players even have a vague uniform to tell the teams apart; it looks like an important event, a tournament between local villages. In fact, it is just a Saturday morning. We wait patiently for someone to score a goal. The goalkeeper does a double save and the ball goes out for a corner kick. The referee blows the whistle, and before allowing the corner to be taken (a rusty bin improvises as the corner flag), he stops the game and allows us to drive through.

Our appointment with the boatman is at the Hotel Alcatraz, a charming cluster of little houses built around a green patio where breakfast is being served. The boatman, Daniel, arrives wrapped up in a thick jumper, yellow waterproof jacket and wellington boots. He introduces himself and recommends we wrap up warm. 'Trust me, it's cold in the middle of the bay.' We follow his jeep. He stops off at home, attaches the trailer with the boat and we reach the long grey beach by the brackish water. Sea and lagoon blend into each other, thousands of birds rummage in the sand in search of molluscs, and Daniel reverses the entire trailer with the boat straight into the water. We go out to sea at high speed, the launch goes nose up, and for at least an hour we hold on tight to the edge, trying to cushion ourselves from the bumps that are tough on the kidneys. When he finally slows down, Daniel Infante tells me that he has been doing this job for 13 years: whales are the tourist resource of Bahía Magdalena for three months of the year. During the remaining nine months he is a fisherman, like everybody else in Puerto San Carlos. The first whales to arrive in January are the younger and stronger males that scour the entire bay and evict any sharks and killer whales, to ensure that pregnant females are not in any danger during delivery. The water is dark; the sun rises in bursts, turning it silver in the light, and Daniel takes note of the changes in colour on the surface, to spot any emerging whale in advance. He holds out an arm and points: a second later, the huge head adorned with white concretions rises up and observes us, while standing in a perfect vertical position. Within minutes, the place is swarming with backs and tails, while we are dumbfounded before this worrying majesty, before this sheer power that could, if it wanted to, just sweep us off with a light flick of a fin – but does not.

My wife Gloria is as entranced as I am but says nothing, sitting stiffly on the middle bench, as though afraid. I think I understand her state of mind: it is an unparalleled emotion, the sense of feeling something atavistic, primordial, that we cannot get our heads around. It is the worry that comes over us when rationality cannot explain something. Here we are, miserable humans from the 20th century, landed by chance in the 21st century – the worst period in the history of relations between our species and Mother Nature – standing before the calm and self-assured movements of these huge and delicate creatures, and we feel small and guilty, the unwilling heirs of unforgivable crimes, and unfortunately equally aware that we are powerless. We are so used to explaining everything with reason that we cannot accept the fact that the vast majority of phenomena that happen in life – and our own lives – cannot be explained.

As usual, when I travel, I have a few books with me, that 'shed light on my path'. More specifically, I am reading *Among Whales* by Roger Payne, a leading expert on the subject, who has devoted his entire life to studying, being with, and especially learning from the largest mammals on the planet. He writes, 'It is because whales are such grand and glowing creatures that their destruction for commerce degrades us so. It will confound our descendants. We were the generation that searched Mars for the most tenuous evidence of life but couldn't rouse enough moral outrage to stop the destruction of the grandest manifestations of life here on earth.'

If the current whale massacres are limited to a few isolated cases of obtuseness on the part of some Japanese or Norwegian maniacs, and the occasional clandestine killing by Russians and Icelanders, the real danger no longer comes from explosive harpoons but from the wicked lifestyle that leads us to treat the ocean like a huge waste dump, where little by little, the food chain is poisoned, from the smallest creature to the largest. Cetaceans, which are at the end of the chain, absorb the worst of it. At the root of it all is always financial profit, including that which is derived from the clandestine disposal of toxic waste, and also the daily use of pesticides and the endless list of polluting substances which sooner or later end up in the sea. We have made the economy our one and only supreme goal, and to hell with the rest, whales included. Roger Payne writes, 'Using an economic argument as if it were the soundest basis for judgment is, of course, at the root of the tragedy of our times. One could hardly find a clearer example of what such reasoning leads to than the present state of whales. Simply stated, putting economics first is the myopia of this, the most short-sighted of all civilizations. It is the view for which our era will be remembered the longest, the addiction for which we will someday be judged more harshly than the most ignorant and prejudiced medieval society. They had an excuse: they simply didn't know any better, whereas we do know better. We have access to the data that proves our folly but because it says uncomplimentary things about what we have become accustomed to accept as "normal", we won't pay attention to it. The ultimate expression of our madness is that we revere as wise those who put economic considerations above all else and sneer at those who see the madness of such a system of values, labelling them as unrealistic.'

9

What Little I Know of Them

WHALES HAD BEEN LEADING a peaceful existence for tens of millions of years before the first hominid assumed the erect position. Even now, studies of their 'customs and traditions' could be summarised in a single sentence: the behaviour of whales constitutes an unfathomable mystery.

We know that they possess a brain more complex than ours, and that they use various languages to communicate at distances unthinkable for human beings. However, unlike us, they use their intelligence for everything except domination and destruction. They are able to use violence in self-defence, if it is called for, and yet there is no recorded case in human memory of an unprovoked attack. To give a concrete example, in the three huge sanctuary bays of Baja California, interaction with grey whales has never caused a boat to capsize – not even 'accidentally'. Yet when Jacques Cousteau was still a young sea explorer and was trying to stick a small harpoon into whales in order to follow their journeys at a distance through a transmitter, in at least two cases the whale that had been 'pricked' turned back and 'punished' them by lifting the rubber dinghy into the air. On one occasion, perhaps because the 'prick' had been painful and had been inflicted immediately after the whale had come up close with affectionate and cheerful curiosity, the whale squeezed Cousteau's colleague, the one who had pricked it under its fin, and dragged him away, holding onto him just long enough for the man to think his end was nigh. Then, most generously, the whale let him go and resurfaced, and while the hapless man was desperately catching his breath, it remained there to watch him, as if asking if he had learnt his lesson. Whales are discerning, and can tell humans apart and, every so often, seem to want to teach us how to behave in this world.

One of Creation's most fascinating mysteries is the song of humpback whales. In the large whale family, the humpback's size is 'average' – the male reaches 17 metres in length, and the female, 19 – while its 'eldest cousin', the blue whale, reaches 26 metres and weighs 130 tonnes. The *Megaptera Novaeangliae*, however, has other reasons behind its supremacy, namely the largest pectoral fins of any other species of cetacean – its name means 'great winged one'. It likes to leap, combining power and grace, and performs impressive moves on the sea surface. Moreover, its fins help to disperse the heat in waters that are too warm for other whales, since it is the only whale that crosses the Equator, going from one hemisphere to the other. And the males ... sing. Nobody has been able to work out why exactly. The assumption is that it is a way of capturing the heart of their companion before mating, or a method of communication, or simply because they just love doing it, the same way we love music and bel canto. We do not even know how they produce those melodic sounds, with which part of their bodies, or if they use air, since they emit their song with their mouths shut and without letting out a single air bubble.

The song of the humpback is a sequence of long and complex sounds that can go on for anything from half an hour to two days in a row. Themes are divided into frequently recurring phrases, or initial improvisations that leave room for perfect 'refrains' of melodies known to the singer's entire group. They can sound like a ballad or stretch into a symphony, ranging over at least seven octaves, with intervals very similar to those used on the scales by our human composers. They have a rhythm that mixes elements of percussion with pure tones equal in proportion to those found in symphonies, and the structure of every song is similar to our own compositions: the creation of a theme, elaboration and development, then a return to the original theme with possible variations. In addition, a fact that causes dismay among experts is that humpback whales use rhyme in their songs and follow a complex series of rules that correspond to our musical conventions. On top of that, obviously, they have their successes as well as their fiascos. A tune taken up by other humpbacks with successive variations and improvisations – they are experienced jazz players – is destined to last, whereas those tunes no one picks up and develops just get forgotten. It all depends on the musical talent of the particular animal and on the tastes of the 'moment', which can last years or centuries.

The song of the humpbacks can be heard from a sailing boat or from a motorboat with the engine off, and the songs take us back to some sea myths, when sailors used to tell of melodic sounds rising from the abyss – the most famous being the one handed down by Homer about the sirens that bewitched Ulysses. For a long time – millennia, in fact – seamen have described singing that was bewitching, haunting, capable of leading the mind astray and of capturing the heart. Even nowadays, the power of the humpbacks' song on the emotions of sensitive people is such that many researchers, whilst recording it, are moved to the point of tears. The musical compositions of humpback whales are extraordinarily similar to ours, except that they were creating theirs for millions of years before us. It can therefore be deduced that the two species developed the same tastes independently and the same basic rules for music composition, except that we got there second. We cannot even tell scientifically why music triggers emotion in humans, but it is astounding to have to admit that the emotions felt whilst listening to Mozart, Bach or Beethoven should depend on compositions and laws, on rhythm, sound, scales and so forth, which is something humpback whales have known from before apes evolved into humans.

We may not know it for a fact, but we sense the songs' importance. Voyager I and Voyager II, the pair of spacecraft sent out to roam the solar system for centuries and millennia, carry aboard a collection of recordings of human voices with greetings in 61 languages, including all kinds of music from Bach operas to African choirs, songs and ditties. One can only picture the expression of an alien who could potentially come across a Voyager and listen to Bill Haley and his Comets. It was all selected by a committee presided over by Carl Sagan, who called it 'the launching of this bottle into the cosmic ocean': myriad emitted sounds, assembled into compositions or melodies created by human beings. Among them there is just one other example of music produced by another mammal: aboard the Voyager, there are also recordings of humpback whales singing.

It is no small step towards understanding these mysteries. It is as though we want to tell the cosmos; we have done all this, we are able to send spaceships into sidereal space and to create languages and music. However, we have other beings here with us – whales, about whom we know little, so perhaps you could also try and understand just how evolved they are. So we are sending you their songs. We find them bewitching, but who knows, perhaps you will understand them better than we do.

Cetaceans are sociable animals (the same is said of humans but all you have to do is live in a block of flats to start doubting that), that form groups without the need for a hierarchy, and that in itself is enough to prove that they are more evolved than we are. The *Odontoceti*, or those with teeth, such as sperm whales, dolphins and killer whales, form more numerous social groups, while the *Mysticeti*, or those with baleens – huge 'brushes' that filter the tiny organisms on which they feed – prefer to live with only a few other individuals, often no more than ten. However, every so often, they congregate in hundreds for brief periods, in a sort of general assembly to discuss something that is known only to them. Apart from the sperm whale, all whales are *Mysticeti*, for example the grey whale, the North Atlantic right whale, and the common rorqual, the blue whale, which is increasingly rare in Greenland, and all those whales we managed to wipe out over the past two centuries – no more than the blink of an eye in the history of those who have populated the seas for at least 26,000,000 years. Their social life is so complex it requires 'nursery schools', for example in the case of sperm whales, where adult females are in charge of bringing up the young and teaching them, thus forming lasting bonds and a powerful spirit of solidarity. There are even 'bachelor schools' where older and more experienced males teach the young ones to become 'men of the world'. They almost certainly use practical examples, but probably also language – except that we are not yet able to understand and decipher it. Perhaps we never will be able to, given that the speed with which we are destroying the planet leaves us no time to understand the whales' teachings.

What we know for certain is that whales are able to communicate across great distances and have always done so, whereas we had to invent the radio and the telephone in order to do just that, and even then we have yet to reach their current super-sophisticated methods. Besides the natural sonar (which allows them to work out the exact conformation of the ocean floor, coastlines and islands and shows them the presence of flood banks), whales emit low frequency sounds – usually around 20 hertz, but they can get down to barely four hertz, which is practically inaudible to humans – which can reach an intensity of 150 decibels and spread over 100 miles in the sea, even crossing oceans. When from around the 1950s US scientists began studying so-called low frequency blips, someone, never even considering the possibility of their being animal in origin, hilariously suggested that it was the Soviets who were propagating these sounds in the ocean, in order to create 'configurations of stationary waves' able to detect the passage of submarines and to work out their position. For once, Cold War paranoia had a positive result: the US allocated huge sums of money to research on these strange 20 hertz sounds, allowing some biologists to unveil the mystery: that it was the whales. It was the start of the discovery of a different world that we still know little about, but that little is amazing. For instance, if grey whales have a regular yearly appointment in Baja California, others, such as rorquals, are sea nomads and have no usual meeting place. Instead, they fix appointments in specific spots, communicating from extraordinary distances, emitting sounds for days and weeks on end, until they either meet up individually (in the case of a couple), or congregate as a group when one of them has found a large supply of food and shares it with its 'friends'.

This discovery, however, has forced scientists to wrack their brains as to how they manage to distinguish these sounds through the roar of the seas. We are used to imagining the depths of the ocean as a sanctuary of absolute silence. Nothing could be more wrong. That belief was dispelled decades ago. Of course, when Jacques Cousteau and Louis Malle made one of the first submarine documentaries, they called it *The Silent World*, but that was back in 1956. Nowadays, we know that the world beneath the waters is much noisier than the world above water. Besides the infinite number of creatures emitting sounds, there are storms that move masses of water and pebbles violently, producing a deafening racket, and the traffic of boats, with powerful engines or even simple outboard motors, which all create a dense network of noises that mix and blend. That does not even take into account the 'occasional' wars involving bomb explosions and missiles, or the more frequent exercises of so many navies. Basically, how on earth is the whales' extraordinary ear able to make out the calls of fellow creatures in this incessant noise? The only explanation is that they must possess a prodigious memory that registers all the various sounds, stores them, then automatically eliminates any interference, allowing them to distinguish only the ones that are of interest. Moreover, they are able to calculate the distance from the point of emission. Modern human technology is far from being able to manufacture a mega computer capable of anything similar. For the highly evolved brains of whales, this has been normal for millions of years.

Mexican grey whales – Mexican at least by birth and weaning, as well as by their regular return – also emit sounds, but their voices are softer, and since they cannot call out to one another across vast oceans, they have the habit of congregating in the same spots. This has put them at risk of extinction, since it is so easy to slaughter them by the thousand in just three bays in the world. For whales that frequent the glaciers of the Arctic and Antarctic, communicating at great distances obviously means safety. When the ice rapidly spreads and compacts because of winds and storms, it makes it even harder to find a chink in which to surface and breathe, so distant companions use their voices to 'guide' the less fortunate ones towards spots where the ice has yet not closed up.

It is a question of pure and simple solidarity. There is affection amongst the whales. They have affection for us, too, in spite of everything. Even though they have proved capable of resorting to violence (in self-defence) as well as to revenge, they have never done so against human beings. You see, the whales know that we are not all alike, and even though there are plenty of swine, there are many among us who are kindly disposed towards them. Yes – the whales know.

Mexican writer Damel Pupko told me of a voyage to Alaska. At one point during a boat excursion through the ice, the pilot could not find a way out from the midst of the web of canals. It was a shape-shifting labyrinth of ice banks that moved and welded together, blocking the way to the open sea. At a certain point, when the passengers were dumbstruck with anxiety, a whale sidled up to the boat and its body language left no doubt that it was guiding them towards the right canals, pushing them in a specific direction when they were about to go into another that would have only made them go back on themselves. Damel was deeply affected by this experience, because he is convinced that the whale was communicating with him telepathically. 'As it came beside us, taking us to safety, it would often look at me and I am certain I heard what it wanted to tell me: I am taking you away from the ice now, but don't come back here. This isn't your world, and you could die here ... It's not something I tell everyone: who'd believe me? But I know you believe me, since you've had contact with whales. I clearly heard the thoughts of this whale as it stared at me, barely a metre away from the boat. I could have reached out and touched it.'

10

On the Mountains of Sierra La Giganta

WE LEAVE PUERTO SAN CARLOS to return to Ciudad Constitucìon, so that the Dodge Durango can gobble up gallons of *gasolina* and we can each down half a litre of coffee that does not go cold even after half an hour: it is like molten lead. The México 1 goes north until Ciudad Insurgentes, which is also peacefully desolate, and then takes a sharp turn east, climbing up the ridges of Sierra La Giganta. The shape of some of the mountains reminds one of a gigantic woman, and has inspired the name of the mountain chain that forms the backbone of Baja Sur, with peaks 1,800 metres high. *Zopilotes* are circling high above: Mexican vultures are formidable flyers, and seen from down here they even look *hermoso* (beautiful), with those huge wings with spreading tips, just like fingers. It is a shame, really, that the occasional cow carcass on the side of the road (that is why lorries have those enormous buffers), gives occasion to see them as real *zopilotes*: repulsively ugly, with bald heads and grey skin smeared with fluids from the corpse, they hop clumsily on the asphalt but cannot make up their minds whether to fly. They give us annoyed looks with those red eyes of theirs, like possessed creatures, and the magnificent wings we see in the blue sky are now heavy loads that they drag around. Naturally, they are very useful and irreplaceable: without their ability to strip the flesh off bovine, equine and ovine

victims – as well as a multitude of other hapless minor creatures claimed by the *carretera* every night – within just a few
hours, it would not be the fragrance of cactus flowers we
would be smelling in this mountain air that invigorates the
lungs. We go past the Estaciòn Microondas Agua Amarga,
with its relay stations that pick up and diffuse signals from
the continent, then, after an hour of road bends, we begin
our descent towards the Sea of Cortez. The coast begins at
Ensenada Blanca where you can see the small Isla Monser-
rat and behind it, Santa Catalina. Then, besides a multitude
of tiny islands and the little Isla Danzante, rises the vast Isla
Carmen. That is what John Steinbeck meant when he wrote
about a 'mirage effect': it is hard to tell where the Baja peninsula ends and where another island – large or small – begins.
It is all a continuous superimposition of layers of desert that
have become detached from the coast.

'As you pass a headland it suddenly splits off and becomes
an island, and then the water seems to stretch inward and
pinch it to a mushroom-shaped cliff and finally to liberate
it from the earth entirely so that it hangs in the air over the
water. Even a short distance offshore one cannot tell what
the land really looks like. Islands too far off, according to the
map, are visible; while others which should be nearby cannot
be seen at all until suddenly they come bursting out of the
mirage. The whole surrounding land is unsubstantial and
changing.' Steinbeck travelled by boat along the Baja coast
in 1940 with his biologist friend Ed Ricketts, in order to subsequently write *The Log from the Sea of Cortez*, in which he
describes a peculiar expedition in search of crustaceans and
small molluscs. The book is dedicated to Ricketts, who died
a few years later, and actually begins with his car being hit by
the Del Monte Express at a level crossing near Cannery Row.

A huge sign points to a somewhat noteworthy place:
Puerto Escondido. Not the one I know well, further south,
on the coast of the state of Oaxaca, but another Puerto
Escondido, forgotten rather than concealed. It is a charming

bay, with many caravans, campers and houses scattered on a network of roads that do not seem to lead anywhere – the ruins of an abortive tourist complex (and I feel like saying 'fortunately so'). It is a sign that the intentions of investors and local politicians have failed in the silent quietude of this still place. The petrol station attendant tells us that the abandoned building, with windows like the hollows of stacked-up skulls, should be finally knocked down. The tiny new tourist harbour, completed a couple of years ago, is semi-deserted, but there are those who hope it might, in a bright future, become a destination for tourists in search of peace and quiet. Meanwhile, the land is divided up into plots, in case anyone should want to buy them.

Pelicans stand in a row on the railings of the pier, believing they are urban pigeons, and the occasional holiday-maker seems happy with the failed developments: they enjoy the quiet and stroll with no rush. The gulf waters are unusually tranquil, the sun is setting, and the few boats that are still out there are preparing to spend another night of dead calm. Steinbeck writes, 'Nights at anchor in the Gulf are quiet and strange. The water is smooth, almost solid, and the dew is so heavy that the decks are soaked. The little waves rasp on the shell beaches with a hissing sound, and all about in the darkness, the fishes jump and splash. Sometimes a great ray leaps clear and falls back on the water with a sharp report. And again, a school of fishes whisper along the surface, each one, as it breaks clear, making the tiniest whisking sound. And there is no feeling, no smell, no vibration of people in the Gulf. Whatever it is that makes one aware that men are about is not there. Thus, in spite of the noises of waves and fishes, one has a feeling of deadness and quietness.'

As we leave Puerto Escondido 2, I think of the pelicans that populate it, and of the bleak forecast of biology experts who insist that they are destined for extinction.

Now that I am over half a century old, I sometimes wonder if it is wise to keep reading the books of those few wise men left on Earth, desperate to sound the alarm that it is constantly about to be destroyed, or whether it would be healthier for me to not give two hoots anymore, and just live out what is left to me, in a carefree way.

Take the example of the pelicans: William Weber Johnson, former director of Time-Life and someone with an in-depth knowledge of the biodiversity of Baja California, wrote, even back in 1978, that they were inexorably condemned. Not because of a direct threat from humans – no one shoots pelicans – but because of the dangers in the food chain: farmers use too many pesticides, tons of which flow down canals and rivers, and sooner or later end up in the sea. Industries do the same with toxic substances and heavy metals, especially mercury. Thus, pelicans, like other species, feed on fish stuffed with pesticides and other toxic substances, and for some years now, their eggs have had thinner shells, so a mother pelican's brood often has a tragic end.

Cetologist Roger Payne adds fuel to the fire. At the end of his blood-curdling list of 'organohalogens' increasingly present in the sea (molecules that contain atoms of fluoride, chlorine, bromine or iodine, which derive from pesticides, herbicides, insecticides and the like, in addition to dioxin, hexachlorobenzene, polychlorinated and polybrominated biphenyls, and all the components of the whole stinking family of hydrocarburates and polyaromatics), he talks of weightless and almost invisible 'diatoms' – the smallest plant in the world. In practice, it is a cell enclosed in a microscopic, siliceous skeleton, which absorbs sunlight and floats thanks to a tiny drop of oil. Diatoms are small but plentiful: they constitute the largest vegetable biomass on the planet. Through that damned droplet of oil – you need a microscope to see it – diatoms absorb all the molecules of the above-mentioned vile substances and store them, since they are unable to split them and digest them. Many and increasingly large organisms feed on diatoms, including fish, and in a long series of dimensional steps, they reach the cetaceans, which, on the food scale, absorb from the waters about 25,000,000 times as much pollution as the diatoms. At the end of this death report, Roger Payne states that in 1987, in the North Atlantic, at least half of the entire dolphin population disappeared, as well as 10 per cent of humpback whales. An autopsy on the bodies recovered showed researchers that the planet's most evolved mammals had died because of a compromised immune system caused by polluting substances.

I just upset myself reading these things – also because if I were to give into my primordial instinct, I would quite happily stick a harpoon into the stomach of a present-day whaler just to ask, 'Tell me, how does it feel?' Similarly, for the sake of consistency, I would have to go and break the arms and legs of all the farmers who use pesticides, not to mention the factory owners who pour their rubbish into the rivers. Honestly, if we wanted to guillotine them all, there would not be enough steel in the world to make all the blades ... so we just cannot think that way. Result: we are totally powerless.

Whilst on the subject of agriculture, I recently read in the Mexican daily *La Jornada* of a scientific study that forecasts nothing less than the imminent extinction of bananas. That's right, the same bananas we find all over the place by the tonne. It is a long story and apparently we have reached the epilogue.

Until a century and a half ago, bananas were prolific in the Tropics in countless varieties: they came in all flavours, sizes and colours. Then United Fruit arrived – now known as Chiquita – and 'extracted' just one variety from the forests of Central America – the one called 'Gros Michael' – and wholesalers turned it into the banana for a couple of decades, since they were all alike and all had the same flavour: yellow, creamy and sweet. As Dan Koeppel explains in his *Banana: the Fate of the Fruit That Changed the World*, the multinational corporation imposed monoculture on 'weak' countries, thereby eradicating other varieties. Moreover, when the intensive plantations were attacked by parasites, they simply said, let's just generously spray pesticides from aircraft, even while the pickers were working on the plantations, bless their souls and those of their families. In 1911, the banana magnate Samuel Zemurray decided to turn the whole of Honduras into his own private plantation, employing the services of a character straight out of a gangster film: Guy Maloney, also known as 'Machine Gun', who organised a private army to exterminate any trade unionists or early ecologists. That is where the expression 'Banana Republic', comes from. The same fate awaited the Democracy of Guatemala, where in 1954, President Jacobo Árbenz, freely elected after implementing agricultural reforms, was overthrown in a coup plotted by United Fruit, effectively supported by Eisenhower (and here is a peculiar detail: the CIA at that time was headed by an ex-director of United Fruit ... talk about coincidence) and the military dictatorship that took over exterminated at least 200,000 native Mayas. One can only hope that these damned bananas really become extinct, given the blood trail they leave behind ... apparently, that is about to happen; any time now.

Now biodiversity allows a species to develop defences if ever it is being attacked, but monoculture does not. In the Sixties, the Gros Michel species was destroyed in the Americas by a fungus. Meanwhile, the same multinational company created in its place the Cavendish variety – prophetically named after the privateer – which was a little smaller and less creamy. Oh, well, never mind. Then, in the Eighties, the Cavendish variety also became diseased, shattering the myth of immunity then paraded by the usual agricultural industry Frankensteins. In Africa alone, 60 per cent of the plants died. A progressive contamination is forecast in America. 'Scientists' on the corporation's payroll have been working on the Goldfinger variety – another film baddie: at least they are consistent with names – which should be more resistant. It's a shame the fruit is hard and tart: a banana for slicing into your gin and tonic – but brilliant discovery, well done.

Johann Hari of *The Independent*, who was nominated Journalist of the Year by Amnesty International, sees a parable for our times in the fact that bananas are doomed to extinction: 'For a hundred years, a handful of corporations were given a gorgeous fruit, and to squeeze every tiny drop of profit from it, they destroyed democracies, burned down rainforests, and ended up killing the fruit itself. But have we learned?'

Nothing. We learn nothing. The world should be run by whales. They would know what to do. I watch pelicans, who multiply despite the thin egg shells; I eat one of those tiny Mexican bananas that have slipped through the net of monoculture logic; and I think I can see the spray of a whale, over there, between an island and the changing horizon. And I think that I am very pleased with the half century I have managed to spend here so far, and I shall not be sorry not to be here anymore, when human stupidity will have wiped out pelicans, bananas and whales. It is far from an anguishing thought. In fact, it is a reassuring one. I start the car again.

Back on the federal road, we go towards Loreto, our stop on today's itinerary. Nearing the outskirts, we pass endless golf courses on our right: they call Loreto Bay a settlement of small villas by the sea. In fact, it has an English name, 'Bay': for Mexico has nothing to do with clubs (golf ones, obviously).

And so, finally, here is the 'capital of the two Californias', as is written on the front of the town hall in typical colonial font. It was the capital until 1828, when it was devastated by a hurricane. In any case, with the separatist aims of Alta California on one side and the inclination of local powers to settle in La Paz on the other, it was doomed from the start. The first Jesuit mission in Baja, the church of Nuestra Señora de Loreto, is the guardian of bygone charm, even though, on the front door, a sign brings us back to the problems of 'progress': GOD IS CALLING YOU BUT HE NEVER USES THE PHONE: SWITCH OFF YOUR MOBILE PHONE BEFORE ENTERING.

11

Eclipse and Sausages

L ORETO SPOILS US with an extraordinary event: a total
eclipse of the moon; one of those that happen only once
every 100 years or so. We are in a privileged spot to admire
it: on the terrace of the Hotel Posada de las Flores. It is the
only colonial building here in Loreto besides the church, and
is the work of an Italian, Giuseppe Marcelletti, so it does not
date back to the era of the Conquistadors. In any case, the
hotel is a beautiful architectural jewel; not because it is luxu-
rious, but rather because of the careful details that make it
just like one of the palaces built by Hernán Cortés. Except
for the fact that the restructuring process was performed on
a 20th-century building, which makes it a rare example of
colonial style recreated by contemporary art. I think it looks
excellent. We could have had a horrible beehive made up of
balconies and glass fronts but instead this is a two-storey
building made of dark stone with wooden window frames,
complete with an ornate front entrance with wrought iron
door handles, a patio with a fountain, and an interior decorated with *azulejos* (ceramic tiles).

The terrace looks over the *zocalo*, the main square. Sunset is
a display of sporadic clouds ablaze over palm trees and mountains and a rose-coloured bay. Alberto sets up the tripod.
The moon starts to disappear behind a translucent disc. We
wait for the phase of total darkness. We are lucky: the sky

has often been overcast in the past few days. On the terrace, everyone thanks fate for having granted us such a splendidly clear night, with a clear and black sky, where the full moon stands out in all its luminosity and is being slowly devoured by the shadows. Then a slight mist, and some greyish cirrus clouds that float right over the moon, irremediably blurring the eclipse. There are murmurs of disappointment. I search the sky until I realise that the cloud has a strange pillar-like shape and does not originate from the vast horizon of the Sea of Cortez but from below, from the earth's crust, from the Baja's surface. In fact, it seems to be generated nearby, in Loreto. Even worse: it is coming from the neighbouring area.

It is the dense and fragrant smoke of an enormous barbeque. The air now smells of sausages and cutlets. The eclipse has been obscured not by a whim of the skies but by the naive carelessness of a merry band who does not give two hoots about either cholesterol, or an event which, when it occurs again, will find us transformed by time into shadows and dust.

To start with, we are so astonished by the discovery of the sacrificial pyre of sausages that no one takes a photo of the culminating moment. Then we start laughing and go and drink a Pacifico *bien helada*. That's right*, como México no hay dos* (There's nowhere like Mexico!). *Salud.*

12

The Charm of Bahía Concepcíon

WE LEAVE AT DAWN to go on an excursion into the heart of Sierra La Giganta, among gigantic cereus cacti and walls of smooth rock. On the way, we give a lift to an elderly man, complete with sombrero and stick – laden with bagfuls of empty cans. I examine him, wondering what on earth he is going to do with them, but what draws my eye is his weather-beaten face, covered in a cobweb of wrinkles, making it impossible to guess his age. His name is Jesús Salvador Velis, and he is the octogenarian patriarch of a large family that manages a *hacienda* (ranch) in the mountains, where they cultivate lemon and olive trees, as well as raising a few head of cattle. 'But my children are scattered in different Mexican states. There are only a few still living with me and I doubt my grandchildren will stay on,' he tells me in a faint voice, accustomed to all-day silence. If I understand correctly, he has 11 children and hordes of grandchildren.

We leave Don Jesús at a fork in the road. He shakes hands to say goodbye, and clambers up a path with the help of a stick as old as he. We keep going until we reach the mission of San Javier de Viggé Biaundó, the original name given by the Guaycuras, which means 'high ground on the canyon'. The Jesuits would impose the name of a saint on each mission, but always also keep the native name as well. The mission was founded by Francisco Maria Piccolo in May 1699.

Subsequently, Father Miguel de Barco had a church built following the design of a Latin cross between 1744 and 1758. This was the first church to have stained-glass windows and prized *retablos* (alterpieces) imported from Tepozotlán, not far from Mexico City. Nowadays, about 100 people live here and there is even a police station: they have displayed on the outer wall a touching poster listing the rights of children, drawn by children who, among other things, ask for their need to play outdoors to be respected and not to be overloaded with homework.

Here, we find California's oldest olive trees, extraordinarily twisted and knobbly; authentic monuments to survival against droughts, the torrid summer heat and the icy winter nights. There are also the grapevines. The first wine, the first in the whole of North America, was made in this mission and if nowadays the US wine business is blossoming and exporting around the world, I doubt that any Californian producer knows that it all began in a remote mission founded by an Italian Jesuit who brought a sack containing roots and vine on the back of a mule.

On our way back, we stop off at the home of Raúl de los Santos, Sierra La Giganta's most knowledgeable guide. He organises excursions on mule-back, for groups willing to stay out for a couple of days or even a week, at night camping by the fire to keep away pumas. As for coyotes, they never come near humans, at least not healthy ones. Raúl tells me that it is difficult to see a puma, but much easier to come across deer and foxes, as well as the odd *borrego cimarrón*, a wild sheep very similar to the ones in Sardinia, but with bigger horns. Of course, rattlesnakes are dangerous, but the mules know how to avoid them, and from what Raúl says, they never get frightened: when they come across one up close, they stand still and wait for the rattlesnake to go back into its den. Baja mules are legendary for their strength and endurance, and for their great dexterity in mountain passes where no hiker would venture on foot for fear of ending up on a precipice.

Apparently, they are the descendants of a native breed of wild donkeys: when mares are on heat, their owners usually set them free in areas where they have seen the donkeys to get them mounted; then they get them back and wait for them to give birth to these solid and powerfully-muscled mules. When we say goodbye, Raúl tells me he has a connection with our country: his daughter-in-law is Italian. However, Raúl too is a man of few words, so I do not ask him to explain how an Italian girl managed to meet his son in these unreachable mountains, and marry him. We resume driving along the Federal 1, going towards the most spectacular panoramic stretch of road of the entire trip, which flanks the bays and coves of Bahía Concepción. At one stage, we stop at a military road block. These are fixed positions. In practice, they are camps for a few dozen soldiers who conduct brief searches, looking for weapons and drugs. The sergeant asks where we come from and where we are going, and when he discovers we are Italians, wants to know which team I support. An Italian who is not a football fanatic seems inconceivable to him. So Alberto steps in with effusive praises of Bologna, who won yesterday, and are confidently heading towards the Premier League. The sergeant shakes his head, not convinced: a team with a name like Bologna – which, in Mexico, has two claims to fame: *spaghetti a la boloñesa* and the *boloñesa*, which is a kind of local mortadella – cannot be taken seriously. In the end, sergeant, corporal and soldiers wish us '*buen viaje y suerte*,' ('Safe travels and good luck') and we resume our journey.

A couple of months ago, the federal government gave the army the task of unleashing a relentless war against the cocaine cartels, after several members of the police force suffered in violent shoot-outs with narco-militia. All the newspapers mention the infamous Los Zetas, ex-military from special departments and death squads from Central America who, left jobless since the advent of democracy in various countries, have joined the private militia of the cartels.

Among them there are many Kaibiles, Guatemalan assault troops responsible for countless Indios massacres. There are also mercenaries – not all of them with latino traits, since some of these are leftovers from those 'advisors' sent down from the north to fight the various guerrillas from Colombia to El Salvador – who now receive 100 times their normal salaries from the cartels. The job of tackling these is hard to assign to ordinary police: the militias are trained to use all kinds of weapons and explosives, have access to a powerful arsenal, assault weapons and grenade launchers. However, since they have been confronted by special branches of the Mexican army, most shoot-outs have ended in the killing or capture of various Zetas. Unfortunately, some soldiers have deserted their ranks: they say that a handful of 'leather heads' were sent first to the US, and then to Israel, to take part in 'special training sessions'. Once back home, they went missing, apparently recruited by a cartel.

And so here we are, lapping up the splendid Bahía Concepcíon: one white beach after another, punctuated by caravans – Playa Buenaventura, Coyote, Requesón, Armenta – and on the surface of these clear waters, I notice an odd stain of vermillion red. My heart sinks ... can someone have possibly poured paint into the sea? But no, they are algae, and I imagine that is why the Spaniards called it Mar Bermejo, or vermillion, before calling it the Sea of Cortez, because they saw that it was streaked with red. Either that or, according to other versions, it was simply because at sunset, it looks like a flow of molten lava. In front of the large bay, there is a kind of long, mountainous peninsula that forms the Sierra Los Gavilanes.

After several kilometres of rock and sand, the arid landscape unfolds into a large oasis, and a stretch of African palm trees as far as the eye can see, fed by a river, the Arroyo de Santa Rosalía or Río Mulegé. We are welcomed at the Mulegé mission by a very young Mexican priest. When he finds out where we are from, he lights up and points to the church, 'It's

dedicated to your saint, Rosalia, patron saint of Palermo!'
And he invites us to Mass, surrounded by hordes of boys and
girls who are about to sing in the choir. He kindly agrees to
Alberto's request that the van be moved so that a photo of
the mission can be taken without vehicles cluttering the view.

Naturally, the palm trees were brought over from southern Spain by Jesuits, and even nowadays, dates are Mulegé's
principal resource. Here, too, we come across various *extran-
jeros,* (foreigners), not tourists but residents, often people of
an advanced age who enjoy the total quiet of the oasis com-
fortably situated in the cove that leads to the sea. There is
a peculiar museum in Mulegé, in the old territorial prison,
which stores various finds: machines for shelling cotton,
ancient underwater equipment and weapons from the colonial era. The strangest of them all is a US rocket, branded
Boeing Delta II, which fell with a crash onto a ranch near
some buildings. Luckily, it did not kill anyone, but if it had
landed on the oasis ... Saint Rosalia, please protect us from
the wickedness of those who launch metal scraps into the air,
which are then likely to fall down on someone else's head.

While we are on the subject of cumbersome neighbours
from the north, it is hard to imagine in this sunny and silent
peace, in this mane of palm trees swaying in the breeze, the
echoing of ghosts, the crack of gunshots and the screams of
the wounded, in the fierce battle that took place on 1 October
1847 between the armed inhabitants of Mulegé and the US
Marines.

13

The Battle that Changed the Destiny of Baja

I T ALL BEGAN IN TEXAS. In 1821, Mexico was becoming
independent after long and bloody wars against Spanish
colonialism, which had wiped out all those who are now
considered Fathers of the Nation. The principal among these
was the priest Miguel Hidalgo. After raising the banner of
the Blessed Virgin of Guadeloupe, he told the insurgents to
gather, and after some initial success on the battlefield, he
too was captured and beheaded without seeing his dream of
freedom come true. In the meantime, in the immense northern territories, various originally Anglo-Saxon settlers had
obtained vast concessions from the Spanish government,
and in 1822, Stephen Austin led many families into Texas in
order to create agricultural and livestock-rearing settlements.
The new Mexican government did not stand in their way,
but considered them an asset, in part because those territories were inhabited by many Apache, Kiowa, Wichita and
Comanche communities who attacked Franciscan missions
and the few Mexican farmers. Therefore, increasing the
'Tejas' population with settlers was deemed to be an antidote
to the raids. They mistakenly believed that the US families
would gradually become integrated into Mexican society. A
fatal error.

Forty thousand acres for just 40 dollars: that was the price
agreed by the Mexican government for the *tejanas* (Texan)

lands. Thousands came down from the North. In 1827, there were 12,000 North Americans; in 1837, over 30,000, compared to only 8,000 Mexican inhabitants. The first problems arose with the 1829 law which forbade slavery: in fact, many North American settlers had brought their slaves with them and continued to exploit them, ignoring the legislation of the host country. That is not all. The settlers refused to pay taxes and went around armed, even though that was forbidden by Mexican law. Meanwhile, in Washington, there was talk of 'Manifest Destiny', which, according to the new middle classes of the West Coast, sanctioned the superiority of the Anglo-Saxon race over the Latin one, and its right to dominate the southern territories. This developed into the Monroe Doctrine of 'America for the Americans', which called for the subordination of the entire continent to the interests of the United States. All this was backed by fierce campaigning by the newspapers in the main cities – from New York to Boston, and from Philadelphia to Baltimore – which portrayed Mexicans as lazy, useless and drunk half-bloods who had inherited from the Indios the worst of indolence and perfidy ... and who, on top of everything else, were Catholics. They involved religion in a 'crusade' in reverse. Brandishing Bibles, Protestant Texan settlers were convinced they were on a divine mission: unfarmed land was an outrage against the Lord, and if Mexicans did not farm it, it should be taken away from them, either peacefully or by force. When the government tried to implement the law against the illegal carrying of weapons, the Texan settlers began shooting at any official who tried to disarm them. On 2 March 1836, Sam Houston, who had given up on a political career in Tennessee in order to settle in Texas, proclaimed the State's independence from the federal Mexican government, becoming the head of the settlers' militia.

Unfortunately, it was Antonio López de Santa Anna who was governing Mexico. He was a former general who had crossed over from the Spanish army to join the independence fighters and had turned into an ambitious politician, a far cry from the statesman the country needed in that situation. He assumed command of the army and marched on Texas. That journey alone was enough to spell failure for the enterprise: a march of thousands of kilometres across mountains and desert for ill-equipped troops, who had almost all been recruited from a young Republic that was struggling to strengthen its position and recover after the bloodshed of the Independence wars. Somehow, 3,000 soldiers managed to reach Texas and lay siege to the fortified mission of San Antonio de Baxar, known as El Álamo, or 'the poplar', where 200 armed settlers, under the command of Colonel William Barrett Travis, had barricaded themselves. The settlers held fast for 13 days but ended up having to yield as they were heavily outnumbered by their enemies. And so the legend of the 'Martyrs of Alamo' was born.

Nowadays, we know that those 'heroes' were a motley band of murderers, slave traffickers, alcohol and arms traders, cattle thieves and desperados. Nevertheless, the moment was fixed in time, and Texas earned its epic and its watchword, 'Remember the Alamo!'

A fierce rush towards Texas was unleashed in the United States. Hordes of volunteers loaded with weapons and ammunition and, most unfortunately, an impromptu army of avengers, under the command of Sam Houston, caught part of a Mexican contingent where Santa Anna, the president, happened to be. It made history as the battle of San Jacinto, and it was a massacre. Santa Anna was captured by the Texans, who forced him at gunpoint to sign at least two 'treaties' – as if anyone could truly negotiate in those circumstances. The papers sanctioned the withdrawal of Mexican troops south of Río Bravo and of course the independence of Texas.

The Mexican parliament refused to ratify an agreement imposed at gunpoint. The US government recognised Texas as a 'sovereign state' but did not want to accept it into the

Union because that would have rocked the political balance and given support to the slave-trading states, who were in a minority in terms of population but not in terms of territory. John Quincy Adams saw an ill omen in that heated controversy. It was early days, but the slave question would end in the Civil War, even if the real reason for the conflict was purely economic, with the industrialised north setting itself against the reactionary landowners of the south. Some of the brightest minds were, in fact, afraid that Texas would tip the balance. Meanwhile, Mexico had to defend itself against a series of vultures attracted by its open wounds: France sent a fleet to bombard Vera Cruz, and tried to invade under the pretext that French properties had been confiscated with the advent of independence. Santa Anna, who had been exiled for having embarrassed himself, returned once again to lead the army, and defeated the French troops, but lost a leg, shot by a cannon. In Yucatán, the Indios, treated like slaves by the heirs to the Spaniards, rebelled: consequently, trade with Mexico City was becoming increasingly difficult, and the capital was at the end of its tether. In addition, all the foreign powers demanded the immediate repayment of all loans secured abroad, dragging the country to the edge of bankruptcy. It was 1844, and in Washington James K Polk had just been elected President on a ticket that promised the annexation of Texas, which was ratified in 1845.

Mexico announced that annexation would be tantamount to a declaration of war. And so it was. Aside from satisfying the desire of unruly Texan murderers, the aim was to conquer spots with the potential for good trading, such as Santa Fe, or established commercial successes, such as California. To save face, President Polk offered Mexico 5 million dollars for New Mexico – which had not yet been named as such – and another 25 million for California. Take it or leave it. There was an outcry in Mexican public opinion and the government refused. Polk was relieved. This way, he could send over the army and save 30 million dollars of public funds.

The command was entrusted to General Zachary Taylor, who led an initial regiment to the south of Río Nueces, which then marked the border between the two countries, and set up a huge military camp in the Mexican village of Corpus Christi. Old Zack, as his soldiers called him, pushed further south, and even had a fort built on the shores of Río Bravo – which was already called Río Grande in the north – drawing up large artillery divisions. On 25 April 1846, a squadron of Mexican cavalry forded Río Bravo and clashed with a contingent sent by General Taylor. Eleven US soldiers were killed in the battle and five were wounded. It was the beginning of the Mexican-American War. It would end on 2 February 1848 with total defeat for Mexico. The cadets of the Colegio Militar of Chapultepéc, the last ones to die, would be forever known as the Niños Héroes, giving their names to streets and squares. The US troops camped out in the historical centre of Mexico City. Volunteer militia engaged in all sorts of looting, rape and crime. Among them, the most ruthless were the infamous Texan Rangers. Moreover, half the Mexican territory was annexed, including California, Arizona, New Mexico, Nevada, Colorado, Utah, Kansas, Wyoming and, naturally, Texas. The daily *New York Herald* wrote of Mexico, 'Like the Sabine virgins, she will soon learn to love her ravishers.'

The Mexicans had engaged in so many battles in the attempt to stop the advance of invaders that they had a far superior artillery; they owned breech-loading guns as opposed to old-fashioned muskets, and their weapons were modern and large compared to the antiquated and sparse equipment on the other side. The peak of the resistance took place in the convent of Churubusco, at the gates of the capital. At the end of a day of attacks and counterattacks, General Pedro Anaya decided to at least save the wounded by raising the white flag. Handing his sword to General Twiggs, he was asked where the ammunition was stored. Anaya replied, 'If we had any ammunition left, you would not be here.'

All the battles were lost, except for the one at Mulegé.

From the start of the conflict, the US Navy had occupied the ports of San Francisco and San Diego, easily conquering Alta California. As for Baja, depopulated and with inadequate garrisons at best engaged in maintaining public order, it was assumed to be easy to invade without a fight, and in September 1846, the gunboat USS *Cayne* entered the harbour of La Paz. When the troops disembarked, they met no resistance, and the Mexican government surrendered, asking that inhabitants and properties be respected. The *Cayne* set sail to go and patrol other ports on the Sea of Cortez. Lieutenant Colonel Henry Burton took up office in La Paz, assuming the role of governor, bringing along a battalion of New York volunteers who, within days, engaged in all sorts of crime, attacking the local civilians. Historian María Eugenia Altable, from the Universidad Autónoma de Baja California Sur, is the author of an in-depth essay on those events, describing them as 'ruthless and bloodthirsty people.'

However, while the invaders were occupying La Paz and San José del Cabo, other small, inhabited places put up resistance. The inhabitants of Mulegé collected all the weapons available in order to form a militia, and sent the Sonora government an urgent appeal. Sonora sent a platoon of soldiers under the command of Captain Manuel Pineda, who was familiar with Mulegé and who quickly gathered the few available resources to defend the town. On 1st October, the corvette USS *Dale* entered the harbour, flying the British flag by order of Captain Thomas Selfridge. Having discovered the ruse, and feeling that he was being called upon to exercise neutrality, Captain Pineda responded with the despatch, 'This place is defended by Mexican forces which I have the honour to command and never will it remain neutral or inert in the face of an unjust war by the United States against the Mexican Republic. We are ready to fight and will do so for as long as we have a drop of blood left. If we have not opened fire yet and are negotiating, it is because you have been cowardly and presented yourselves under the British flag.'

At that point, the corvette's cannons shot at a schooner moored in the port, which had already been abandoned by the defending forces. The following morning, 2 October, Marines disembarked on board boats, and were decimated by bursts of gunfire raining down on them from the thick palm groves. Covered by shots from the ship's guns, they managed to line up in spots along the cove and in the suburbs of Mulegé, but after eight hours of fierce counter-attacks, they were pushed back by the Mexicans, and the corvette went out to sea. This example inspired many more – and proved it was possible to vanquish the powerful enemy. Militias sprung up everywhere – from Loreto to San Ignacio, and from Todos Santos to Comondú – often lead by priests, like Vicente Sotomayor, who waged guerrilla warfare against the occupiers, causing heavy losses and preventing the complete control of the peninsula. At one point, they even managed to besiege the garrison of San José del Cabo, which had to resort to help from naval units from La Paz. When the war ended, the United States demanded that Baja also be handed over, but the Mexican government managed not to surrender it to them, thanks to the fact that unlike Alta California, it was not militarily occupied. Faced with the prospect of a long and exhausting guerrilla war, Washington gave up: it had already obtained half of Mexico, so it thought it would be better to devote itself to the exploitation of its new territories rather than to waste energy on a semi-desert peninsula deprived of tempting resources. Perhaps we owe it to those volunteers and to Mulegé's few soldiers that Baja is still Mexican.

14

Punta Chivato

W<small>E ARE LOOKING</small> for a corner of paradise. I know, the term is overrated but still ... although Baja has astonishing surprises in store in terms of natural beauty, Punta Chivato is by no means inferior. We keep track of Palo Verde on the map, and when we find a sign – appropriately green – pointing to it, we turn right and venture down a wide track of fine and dusty sand that is much softer than what we have come across up till now. We skid gently from right to left, and our tyres slide without accident as though we are sledging on snow. We stop briefly at a widening in the road which forms the only curve of the entire journey. On the edges of the track, where the 'centipedes' – that is what they call a variety of cacti that practically crawl on the ground – form an insurmountable barrier thanks to hard, sharp thorns like an eagle's talons, there are three crosses with names on them and a few wilted flowers. I have never found out whether they are real graves, that is, if the victims of the accident are really buried there on the roadside, or whether they are symbolic reminders of where and when the tragedy took place. You come across so many crosses like that in Baja, or sometimes small headstones with the dead person's photo. However, when you look at them closely, they look like actual tumuli and not just like memorials of an unlucky day. It is a mystery how anyone could have possibly died right here, where if you fall backwards, the soft sand absorbs every shock and the cacti are certainly not as unyielding as oaks or plane trees. I would exclude the possibility of these people having been murdered during a robbery or a settling of scores because Baja is one of the most peaceful places in the world – the crime news bulletin is ridiculous here, in comparison with the rest of the country and continent. So I guess they must have been the victims of the only predator that kills humans. Since we no longer have one, we invented one that is more dangerous than tigers and lions: the automobile.

Mindful of that, I drive carefully. After raising dust for a couple of hours, the view unfolds on Bahía Santa Inés, with the island of the same name in front and Punta Chivato stretching like a quiet and gentle dream. It is magical.

The Hotel Posada de las Flores, same name and owner as the one in Loreto, is extraordinarily well positioned, with sea on both sides of the promontory, fabulous dawns and sunsets and an ensemble of low stone buildings immersed in a kind of Zen garden, punctuated with cacti and rocks of pink granite. North-Western Sardinia must have been like that before it became the Costa Smeralda … except that this is much more scarcely populated and rarefied. Around here, too, the land has been divided into plots, but what prevails, as far as the eye can see, is boundless space and the absence of human traces.

Giuseppe, the owner of the hotels which would doubtless feature at the top of an ideal league as 'the most beautiful on the peninsula', is a pioneer among Italian tourist operators in Baja. He has ended up settling here, and goes back to Rome only when he really has to, and every time he does, he cannot wait to come back to this secluded spot where life seems to be suspended in mid-air, silent and delicate, and where you get the sense that you need nothing else in the world to feel content. I first met him about 12 years ago, and had not seen him since; now he has become a pilot. He owns a small plane, in which he lands and takes off from a sandy track which has been flattened by a wealthy gringo who has a beautiful house nearby, and who every so often comes here from Los Angeles. 'You cannot imagine what Baja looks like from the sky as you glide between the spurs from one bay to the other,' says Giuseppe. 'Brushing the cacti, looking at a blue whale, which, from up there, looks like an aircraft carrier – no, you cannot possibly imagine what it's like. You must come back and I'll show you some unforgettable things from the plane.'

At this precise moment, unfortunately, I cannot take him up on it. The Cessna is being serviced in Los Cabos; it had a couple of 'tiny pieces' of spare parts to replace. I promise him I will come back to Punta Chivato. Promises of wandering Italians whose paths cross under Mexican skies and who plan to fly over the land. What are such promises worth? Well, who can tell? *Hay más tiempo que vida* (there is plenty of time), but meanwhile, life goes on, and you reach an age where, at times, you feel as though the years are sliding downwards faster and faster, and you acquire that sensible fatalism which allows you to promise 'see you soon' even though it really does not matter when, how or if. *Quien sabe* (Who knows).

Spending time here, chatting to the few Mexicans around, I notice there is a serious problem for anyone trying to start a tourist activity in Baja, and that is the loneliness of the workers. Beside the towns, which are far apart, many dreamlike spots like Punta Chivato must resort to cooks, waiters, cleaners, managers, gardeners and so forth who come from other areas, even from states beyond the gulf. These are workers who at the end of their shifts are alone and deprived of the diversions found in populated places, of the warmth of human contact and of people with whom they have something in common. So they are severely homesick, and find it hard to remain very long in these spots, which to us passing travellers, seem like real corners of paradise. Loneliness gives any salary a bitter edge.

These days in Punta Chivato are unforgettable, but absolute quiet has a limit, after which I feel ready to leave. I turn on the engine of the Dodge Durango. *Adiós*, Punta Chivato. Every time I am happy somewhere, I have got into the habit of asking myself: would I live here?

No.

But it has been wonderful, anyway.

15

Miner Indios and Muralist Indios

S ANTA ROSALÍA IS a common name, and the name of a
town about 60 kilometres from Mulegé, which was the
most densely-populated spot of Baja Sur in the first decade
of the 20th century. That was thanks to the copper mines, so
it is no coincidence that Santa Rosalía is the patron saint of
miners. With its colourful wooden houses and sloping rooftops, it reminds me of little towns in Costa Rica or on Nica-
ragua's Atlantic coast. The main attraction is in the square: it
is the church. Made up entirely of iron, in the midst of all the
timber, it was designed by Eiffel – yes, really – the Parisian
one. The large number of bolts are his unmistakable signa-
ture. As the bronze plaque states, it was built for the Paris
Exposition Universelle in 1889. Taken apart and packed up,
it lay forgotten in a Brussels warehouse until it was purchased
by an engineer who was working in Santa Rosalía at the
time. Having rounded Cape Horn, it completed the perilous
journey back in 1896, the year in which the final bolt was
screwed in. And now it beats time with the toll of its Parisian
bells. Inside, to get around the torrid heat of an iron church
in the midst of a peninsula with a desert climate, there are
countless fans spinning slowly from the ceiling, providing
moderate relief in the semi-darkness barely brightened by
colourful stained glass.

Everything looks French in Santa Rosalía. Even the large

bakery regularly churns out crusty baguettes. The only detail that feels out of place is the *taqueria* on one of the central streets. It is called 'Pavarotti' because of the owner – who, sadly, recently died – who, I am assured, bore a striking resemblance to the great Italian tenor, and who loved the latter's singing so much, he even passed away almost at the same time as his idol.

The French mining group Compagnie du Boleo was founded here in 1885, to exploit copper deposits. The initial 20,000 hectare concession quickly rose to 600,000. Porfirio Díaz had a weakness for Paris, and wanted Mexico City to resemble it with its monuments and architecture, so he did not oppose the people of El Boleo in any way. Even now, the city is divided in two: the lower part is for ordinary people and the upper part – with its more beautiful and airy buildings – is for managers, engineers and technicians. The first part is called Mesa México, and the other, Mesa Francia. It is a clear and unequivocal division.

We are welcomed by Ricardo Mata, who is the head of the cultural department of the city council, based in a beautiful wooden building that has so many windows you can practically see into every hall and room. This building is listed as a UNESCO World Heritage site, just like the old Hotel Central which, Ricardo tells us, saw at the start of the last century the clamorous and lively capture of a famous gringo desperado – a bandit with an extraordinary bounty on his head. He, like so many others, had come South to escape the sheriffs that were after him, and ended up falling into the hands of the Mexican police after a saloon-style shoot-out. Unfortunately, no one remembers his name, whether he was killed during that event, or if he was handed over to the neighbours in the North and therefore hanged, or if he ended his days in a Baja jail, or if he escaped. There is a blank. All that is known of him is the shoot-out at the Hotel Central, which looks like a film set dear to Sergio Leone. Afterwards, we visit the cultural centre, where traditional dance classes are taking place: girls and boys are tapping their heels and toes on a wooden stage. The former are graceful, the latter more manly. They twirl and mime courtship scenes under the severe gaze of the teacher. There are old photos on the walls, which tell of the mining epic of Santa Rosalía: the lean faces and muscular bodies of Yaqui Indians, who immigrated from Sonora and Sinaloa to dig tunnels with a pickaxe; others look smaller and do not have such a proud and indomitable expression: they are natives of Guerrero, who came from further south, and who were probably among the first to die of infection and disease. Deaths caused by such accidents, however, affected everyone, including the many Chinese men who appear in the photos.

Ricardo also takes us to Mesa Francia, where we visit the large administration offices of the El Boleo company, now transformed into a museum, with archives bursting with large registers which collect information, in the form of numbers and dates, on the hardships of thousands of miners who were paid a pittance.

Of course, the French brought progress. They built an electric power station brought over across the sea, and lit the city with countless lamp posts. They installed telephone lines to maintain constant communication between the pits and the offices; they built roads and bridges, and then a modern harbour in order to load the copper and receive supplies. They developed trade, and Santa Rosalía expanded, opening schools, a hospital, hotels and police stations. However, it was a society we would now describe as 'imbued with apart-heid': Mexican miners scarcely had access to those facilities and were, in particular, forced to depend on the notorious *tienda de raya* ('company-owned store'). It was a large empo-rium where miners and their families were obliged to buy everything they needed. They would end up in debt, and very often even began their jobs with debts, which meant they did not receive a salary but had their working days 'deducted' from their bill. El Boleo raised cattle, grew vegetable gardens and extracted drinking water from the wells, thereby creating a closed and self-sufficient society. This resulted in a surrounding area that was backward, and made it impossible for farmers and small breeders to take advantage of the commercial streak in the densely populated town. In fact, many found themselves 'dispossessed' by new concessions, and thrown off their own land. El Boleo went as far as forbidding food shops. Everything had to go through the *tienda de raya*, which kept the miners in debt, and effectively in slavery. Porfirio Díaz would make generous 'concessions' to foreign capitals and cared little about the devastating effect this had on the local population, thus creating the conditions for the outbreak of revolution – the first revolution of the 20th century and the only one that was truly social as opposed to purely 'political'. It is right here in Santa Rosalía that the first murmurs were heard when the miners, exasperated by the high death rate in the tunnels, disease and their social marginalisation, began protesting alongside the ranchos inhabitants. They protested against pollution in the few waterways – where the company poured out production waste – and the gradual disappearance of surrounding forests, cut down to make sleepers, poles and fire wood to feed the boilers. Trade union struggles began, and the museum mentions Benjamín Félix Villanueva, leader of the miners, whose claim to fame, in addition to fighting for the workers' rights, was bringing a cinema to Santa Rosalía. It was called Triatón and was both the headquarters of the trade union and a projection room, where heated meetings alternated with heartbreaking silent films.

We say goodbye to Ricardo and to his wife, who has been to Italy on the invitation of Catholic volunteer associations, and who urges us to come back and visit them whenever we wish – '*Mi casa es su casa*' ('My home is your home').

The road, our beloved Carretera Federal 1 – also known as the Transpeninsular – heads west and penetrates a mountainous desert. Every few kilometres, I notice green bins on the edge of the road. In Baja, refuse collection is a serious and precise matter; the service is efficient even in the middle of the desert.

Once we go past Cuesta del Inferno the landscape becomes arid; vegetation disappears and cacti come to dominate again. The ochre yellow and the red of some rocks transform the luscious greenery of the gulf oases into a faint memory. We enter the Vizcaino Desert, a biosphere reservation, and on our right tower the extinguished volcanoes of Las Tres Virgenes, except that one of them seems to be emitting a column of white smoke. It is a strange optical illusion: a commercial plane has left a trail of condensation right behind the crater and has thus formed an ephemeral eruption cloud. However, there are at least 3,000 or 4,000 metres between the peak and the white streak across the clear sky.

We reach the Mission of San Ignacio Kadakaaman, which means 'stream in a bed of reeds'. Unlike other missions in the heart of the peninsula, San Ignacio has become a town clustered around the church, and has one of my favourite hotels. Desolately large, occupying just the ground floor, it is in effect a courtyard of rooms around a flowery patio. There is no superfluous luxury and no ceremony, the staff are straightforward and not talkative, and everyone is polite and endearingly quirky – passing visitors stay overnight and leave at daybreak to go and see the great mystery enclosed in the heart of Baja California, the rock paintings.

We will never know if they came from the north or from faraway Polynesian islands. The only probable fact is that they populated this area at least 10,000 years ago. They hunted and gathered forest fruits, but were also fishermen. They left us the riddle of these monumental rock paintings – which some scholars attribute to the Comondú civilisation – about which we know, however, very little, apart from a few graves containing skeletons of tall, robust people, a few necklaces, and many arrow points. Perhaps they believed in an afterlife, seeing as they placed everyday objects next to each dead person; things like spatulas and bodkins made from deer bone, in case they came in handy in the next life, or mother-of-pearl pectorals, or flutes carved from pelican bone. The type of graves and the way bodies were laid out implies a complex burial ceremony, something which, according to anthropologists, indicates an advanced level of social organisation. Moreover, they were extraordinary mural painters. We are not talking about simple anthropomorphic figures, or hunted or sacred animals, but about frescoes representing collective scenes, resembling group ceremonies in which stylised men and women raise their arms and are surrounded by deer, wild sheep, pumas, hares and examples of marine fauna – giant rays in particular – or else are superimposed onto them. There is also a wide variety of geometrical and abstract drawings, almost certainly shamanic visions in a state of trance induced with hyperventilation and massive doses of tobacco. In some cases, the figures seem to dance, as the shamans, and whoever else took part in these ceremonies, used to do by following the rhythm until they reached a state of ecstasy or simple daze.

What astounded those who made these early discoveries, and made scholars wrack their brains, are the dimensions of the style known as Gran Mural, and the fact that many rock paintings were drawn about 10 metres from the ground and on cave vaults or the walls of steep rocks, access to which would have required complex scaffolding. Moreover, they used such sturdy substances that some of the colours are still intact, like the red and some ochre trimmed with white. The most ancient ones date back 7,500 years and cover a span of five millennia of almost uninterrupted artistic practice. Furthermore, the areas where at least 250 rock paintings have been discovered so far are quite hard to reach. That is why they are so well preserved. No one saw them until the 19th century. No one except Indios approached by Jesuits, who probably knew these places that they held sacred and where they continued to hold propitiatory ceremonies. And now, they, too, have disappeared. The mystery of the painting-loving civilisation that left these vestiges between Sierra de Guadalupe and Sierra de San Francisco, in an area of over 6,000 square kilometres, will not be solved.

We do not know the meaning of the symbols in these paintings, but we can sense that they speak of mythology, of shamanic powers and images that seem 'abstract' only to us but which are trying to hand down a vision of the world of the ancient Baja inhabitants. We have not found the key to their language, and it is the very fact that it is so magnificently indecipherable and incomprehensible that fascinates us.

16

From the Bay of the Angels
to the Devil's Peak

GUERRERO NEGRO has been the longest and most emotional stay of this journey. After that, we go straight north, as far as the crossroads at Parador Punta Prieta. Here, we veer right down 80 kilometres that cross the Desierto Central from east to west, between the mountain ranges of San Borja and Calamajué, until the strip of dried asphalt goes down to the Sea of Cortez and runs straight into Bahía de los Ángeles.

It is a fishermen's harbour, and owes its existence to the spring that flows out at the foot of the mountain and which populated this area with humans, as demonstrated by the heaps of shells they fed on for at least 6,000 years. Nowadays, its lifeblood is the plentiful amount of fish in its turquoise waters. It is the only natural harbour along 200 kilometres of inaccessible coastline. The bay is protected by a kind of natural barrier made up of islands. The largest is consequently called Ángel de la Guarda, 'guardian angel'; it is only 80 miles from the coast, 68 kilometres long and its mountains reach 1,200 metres in altitude. With no fresh water, it is not inhabited, even though at one stage Kunkaak Indios came this far. They were called *Seris* – 'sand people' – by the Opata Indios and also, therefore, by the Spaniards. They came from the Sonora coast and especially from the nearby Isla Tiburón, still the territory of these native communities who, and this is yet another world mystery, differ from other ethnic groups by being taller (on average 1 metre 82cm) and by their language, which is similar to Tibetan, containing some words with identical meanings and pronunciation. One interesting theory is that groups of Tibetans may have reached Alaska thousands of years before China came to be dominated by Mongolian stock, and then come down from the Bering Strait and populated the American continent. Consequently, the Kunkaaks would be the descendants of indisputably the most ancient inhabitants of the Americas, who remained here after incessant migrations further south, and exiled themselves to Isla Tiburón in order to escape the Spanish conquerors, who never succeeded in subjugating them. Nowadays, the Seris are famous for their well-known and stunning sculptures in *palo hierro*, the world's hardest and densest wood, which comes from a tree in Baja and also grows on the coast of Sonora. In particular, they carve elegant animal figurines – dolphins, whales, turtles, eagles, or owls, as well as the slender *correcaminos*, the roadrunner – the bird that runs but cannot fly. If you come across one, he vanishes in a second, leaving nothing behind but a puff of dust: just like the roadrunner in the cartoon. In my home in Bologna, I have accumulated a wide range of animals carved by the Kunkaaks – including a *correcaminos*. I have bought one during every trip to the desert, as well as a pretty mahogany-coloured cactus, which gives out a light scent of faraway places and nostalgia during the long winters in the Po region.

Bahía de los Ángeles is situated at the narrowest point of the gulf, with a scattering of 50 or so islands, where the flux of the tide creates whirlpools that generate a high concentration of oxygen. This results in rich marine flora and fauna that have no equal in the world and which attract sperm whales and humpback whales from afar, while northern whales stay here all the time. This is probably because they find an extraordinary abundance of food here, not to mention the fact that nobody has had the right to kill them here for over half a century. And so they have become the only 'sedentary', or better, 'geographically stable' – whales, since they actually do move, with a solemn elegance that sets them apart.

In the harbour, the fishing boats, *los camaroneros*, stand side by side, with their large, oblique iron arms used for heaving up tonnes of lobsters, forming a large 'village' which you can cross from one bridge to the next. We have no trouble finding someone willing to take us out for a ride a little further, between the Bay of Angels and the Guardian Angel Island, to see rays and whales. Not too far, though, because the same currents that make this sea so well-stocked with fish can also play nasty tricks on the most skilled sailors. We do not have our playful and affectionate grey friends here, and the huge backs we catch sight of, a few hundred metres away, just stick to their watery path without even giving us so much as a look. Instead, it is a group of joyful dolphins that surrounds us; they have great fun racing the boat, criss-crossing and occasionally emerging to laugh in our faces. I recall my first trip to Baja, when I saw posters advertising a dolphin hunt for the benefit of possible North American customers. I was horrified. How is it possible – I wondered, astounded and offended – that in my Mexico, that is on the frontline of the protection of cetaceans, that someone actually goes dolphin hunting? The ignorance was all mine! Luckily, before I had the chance to lodge a series of urgent complaints to the authorities of La Paz and Mexico City, someone explained to me that, owing to a 'hitch' in the English language, the same word is used for two very different creatures. One is an intelligent mammal; the other, a hapless fish with fine meat. Along this coastline, which plummets steeply 200, then 1000 metres – you barely swim a few strokes before there's nothing beneath you. About 600 types of fish thrive here, and among them swims the said dolphin, or rather, the *Coriphaena Hippurus* or common dolphinfish, which is characterised by its ability to turn all the colours of the rainbow when it is hooked and pulled aboard.

It is a colourful farewell to life, which looks to us like a riot of hallucinogenic reflexes whereas it must be unpleasant, to say the least, for the fish. In practice, it is a traumatic alteration in the balance of chemical substances in the cell which regulate pigmentation. The person responsible for the confusion in the name was privateer Francis Drake's chaplain, who caught one in 1578 and who, in his foolishness, called it a dolphin because he was unable to find an appropriate name for the wonder he held in his hands. Even Lord Byron was so fascinated by this radiant way of dying, that he was inspired to write:

> Parting day
> Dies like the dolphin, whom each pang imbues
> With a new colour as it gasps away,
> The last still loveliest, till 'tis gone and all is grey.

No offence intended to so many translators who, as ignorant as I, no doubt got confused and attributed to Byron an elegy on the death of a dolphin ....

The ones surrounding us now, however, are an ode to life itself. There is no point on my dwelling on their intelligence – I have already talked about the intelligence of whales, which is, in many ways, superior to ours. However, I am not about to miss out on another opportunity to highlight other aspects of our ignorance in this case. Studies and research over the past 30 years have proved that we are still very far from understanding how dolphins can do things that contradict our very laws of physics. For instance, we cannot explain how they can swim 7 times faster than their muscle structure should allow, according to what we know of hydrodynamics, or how swimming at such speed does not cause a vortex and consequently, noise – something which makes them different from any other body, either fish or sophisticated car. Another thing is their language. When they are out of the water – and talking to us humans – they speak using phonemes, whereas when they communicate among themselves, they use low-frequency signals and ultrasound. Doctor Luis Hermann, who has devoted his entire life to the study of dolphin language, established examples of communication and proved that these amazing animals can learn 'human' vocabulary based on gestures, like sign-language, and then manage to understand not only syntax but also the logical meaning or words. If Hermann tells a dolphin, 'take this ball and throw it through the hoop', the dolphin does just as he is told; but if Hermann inverts the gestures and says, 'take the hoop and throw through the ball', the dolphin shakes his head to make him understand that it is nonsense. The problem is not, therefore, in getting dolphins to understand us, but in our understanding what dolphins say among themselves and what it is they wish to say to us.

Then, there is also this alleged 'telepathy': a dolphin can sense the intentions of a man underwater a few seconds before he acts. However, this is because of his 'sonar glance': since the human body is 70 per cent water, the dolphin can 'see through' it, notice in advance if the man is about to tense up a muscle, and prevent it. What is even more fascinating is their ability to bring on a sense of wellbeing: with a simple sonar impulse, dolphins can stimulate our endocrine glands by making them vibrate, and therefore induce a sense of relaxation. That is why, since the Nineties, there has been a rise in 'dolphin therapy' for autistic children in dolphin aquariums. Similarly, by using certain frequencies, dolphins can alter our brainwaves with as yet unknown psycho-physical consequences – though, as far as we know, these animals love us and only use their powers to make us feel better, not worse. There are rare cases to the contrary ... but there are reasons for that. These reasons should be weighed up by an international court for 'crimes against the better part of Creation' i.e. not the human race. In the recent past, both the US and Russian navies have tried to train dolphins for military purposes, for example training them to place mines under hulls, defuse those of others, and even attack 'enemy' divers. We know that a large proportion of these intelligent mammals 'deserted', and, preserving a very negative view of humans, even attacked a few. But these cases are extremely rare. If we consider that for thousands of years, the most evolved civilisations have considered dolphins to be sacred and therefore untouchable and worthy of profound respect, we can conclude that, within the span of known history, we must have reached the pits. Fortunately – unlike dogs, who stupidly keep obeying any human order to attack, no matter how perverse – dolphins have proved to be 'unreliable sol-diers', and creatures we consider 'unpredictable', and so these kinds of experiments are now being abandoned.

We go back to the 'eternal México 1', once again driving north or, rather, north-west towards Cataviña, and cross-ing a different kind of desert landscape. It looks like it has been bombed by huge rounded rocks that are scattered on the side of the road and then it vanishes into the mountains. Hopping from one granite 'ball' to another, we notice a scorpion in a cleft. Alberto claims that in Baja they are not deadly. Ours, although about 12 centimetres long, certainly is not: as we draw closer, we notice it is as dead as a door nail. I stop to watch the ants that have nearly finished stripping off its flesh. In Spanish, it is called an *alacrán*, and is one of the most ancient beings on the planet; still almost identical to how it was 400 million years ago when it emerged from the ocean to adapt to life on earth. And it is not an insect, but the most primitive among arachnids, belonging to the same class as spiders and mites (the species' most unlucky cousins who, instead of enjoying the vastness of the desert, or spin-ning webs fit for a tightrope walker, nest instead in miserable rugs and mattresses. It is a case of 'dust to dust' even while they are alive).

What makes us go back to the car is the thought, 'I don't suppose there are any rattlesnakes here?' Everything I have read about Mexico tells me that scorpions claim more victims here than rattlesnakes, but for some reason, to hear the unmistakeable sound of that vibrating tail is more disturbing than a hundred scorpions scrambling up your walking boots. There are at least 18 different types of rattlesnake in Baja, and the strangest one is the rattlesnake without a rattle. The first specimen was discovered in 1952 by biologists on the Island of Santa Catalina, south of Loreto and so it was called *crotalus catalinensis*. The foremost authority on rattlesnakes, Laurence Klauber, stated that 'a rattlesnake without a rattle cannot be a rattlesnake'. Elementary, my dear Watson. And so according to him, it must have been a rare anomaly, probably due to mutilation. They then found nine more specimens in 1962 and 1964 and no one has any more doubts now. It is, to all intents and purposes, a rattlesnake which has been reproducing without a rattle for a number of centuries. The evolutionary process that has deprived it of the characteristic alarm system that has saved the skins of countless careless desert travellers remains a mystery. *Crotalus catalinensis* wriggles its tail silently, then bites – and probably wonders why its opponent did not get away. 'I did wriggle my tail at you, you know – what do you expect me to do now? It's in my nature, you see...'

After Cataviña, there are just a few houses scattered along the road, and we stop for the compulsory refill right in the middle of Deserto Central, before starting again towards El Rosario. On the side of the road, and even in the thick of the cacti, there are the wrecks of cars and vans. Some of them are not long dead, while others have turned into rusty sculptures which, when all is said and done, do not actually clash with the landscape. They look like drifting wrecks that have run aground in the sand, or scrap-metal pachyderms that have collapsed, exhausted, after a long journey that has lead them all the way here so that they could enjoy the feeling of the engine starting, one last time.

El Rosario, too, has the look of a place you just pass through, and it is only the odd lorry driver that stops here to eat and rest. We are now heading to Ensenada, and the road often brushes the coast, spoiling us with glimpses of glistening ocean. Between Vicente Guerrero and Camalú, the spurs of Sierra San Pedro Mártir start appearing, a view dominated by the majestic Picacho del Diablo, which at 3,095 metres is the peninsula's highest peak and is often snowcapped, as it is this winter. In the distance, pine trees replace cacti but then disappear at high altitude, where all you have is snow and rock. Only *borrego cimarrón* – horned sheep – go up there and the sky is the brightest blue that any human could hope to see with his or her feet on the ground. When photos taken by a US satellite showed Baja California 'Norte' to be the world's least cloudy area, practically devoid of mist because of the dry air, they decided to build an astronomy observatory right here, next to the summit of Picacho del Diablo, at an altitude of 3,096 metres. The Universidad Nacional Autónoma de México built a road 120 kilometres long, between the mountains and canyons, in order to carry up their building materials and equipment, and now the observatory is managed jointly by Mexico and the United States. Entry into the final section, which leads to the buildings, is forbidden. In this perfect atmosphere, free from smog and pollution of any kind – including lighting – even the dust raised by our wheels would disturb this air that is so rarefied and pure.

17

'Ensenada the Dead Seal ...'

A ND HERE WE ARE, back to 'civilisation' again. As we approach Ensenada, built up areas are gradually increasing, with terraced houses for holiday makers, traffic, pick up trucks with Californian number plates, loaded with surf boards, where blondes outnumber brunettes. Pemex distributors – oil is still nationalised in Mexico so it is just Pemex, with no trademarks and one price across the whole Republic – punctuate the view, with increasingly large and brightly-lit service stations.

Ensenada is not attractive, but has the shabby feel of a relaxed amusement park and is made up of more cantinas than discos. The queen of them all is Cantina Hussong's, located in the centre of town, which is infested with shops selling souvenirs and cheap crafts. It was founded in 1892 by German immigrant Johann Hussong, when Ensenada was a fishing village with 5,000 souls. Its claim to fame and its pride and joy is to have given birth to the Margarita cocktail, a creation of Mexican barman Carlos Orozco, who worked here in 1941, when he mixed, in perfect balance, tequila, Damiana (nowadays substituted with Cointreau), Mexican lemon juice (green, small and sour, often confused with lime, which is something quite different, sweeter and more fragrant) and crushed ice, with the final touch of garnishing the rim of the glass with salt. Ensenada, a town that has drawn entire generations of Californian students, who come here to get plastered away from their own country's legal restrictions, was also frequently visited by Jim Morrison, when the latter was still at university. Eventually, having become the voice, mind and accursed soul of the Doors, he commemorated those days in a famous track: 'Ensenada the dead seal ... ghosts of the dead car sun. Stop the car. Rain. Night. Feel.'

The tradition of crossing the border in order to get drunk is an old one and dates back to Prohibition. Nowadays, many tourist spots in Mexico, including Ensenada, await, like manna from the sky, the arrival of Spring Breakers – students who come here for the spring holidays and spend ready cash on alcohol, thanks to Mexican law, which allows drinking from the age of 18, whereas in the States you have to wait until you're 21. However, many young people come here for a different reason: the surfers seem like a breed apart. You hardly ever see them hungover; they are up at dawn to take advantage of the best waves, and congregate again at sunset – then head straight to bed. Between rides, all they talk about is boards, crests and successful or failed enterprises. Still, seeing them in action is like witnessing a fascinating ritual.

At about 12 nautical miles east of Ensenada are the two islands of Todos los Santos, which also lend their name to the bay. The larger of the two is about 15 kilometres long, and although the south side offers some splendid beaches, the twin islands are not a tourist attraction. Instead, they are known to the world's best surfers, especially that handful of lunatics who ride the notorious and much sought-after big waves.

Decades can go by without it happening, and then a storm in the Bering Strait triggers a swell; a sequence of gigantic waves that spread south. And so the best big wave riders – those few surfers capable of sliding over and under them without getting themselves killed – congregate in specific points. They are mainly from Australia, New Zealand, Hawaii and California. There is only one from Mexico: the now legendary 'Coco' Nogales who, needless to say, is from Puerto Escondido (the 'real' one, with a fast pace of life, in the State of Oaxaca). The big wave, which inspired cult films such as *Big Wednesday* and *Point Break*, appeared on 5 December 2008 on the coast of the larger of the two Todos los Santos islands. And so 'they', the big wave riders, were all there, ready to defy waves 18 metres high that lash out two-tonne hammer blows when they break, and are called 'killers' with good reason. Losing your balance could prove fatal, because you could end up in wipeout mode; in other words, knocked over and pushed towards the bottom for over two minutes – long enough to lose your strength in that colossal spinner and drown. Furthermore, a hammer blow in the back almost always knocks you unconscious. Nevertheless, one more time, the big wave riders have managed to make it through in one piece, with no bones broken. Coco Nogales tackled his wave in the usual towing style, which consists in being towed by a personal watercraft – driven by his faithful squire Godofredo – up to the top of the wave. Once he has reached the crest, Godofredo lets go of the rope and the rest is in the lap of the gods. The long, two-metre board slides down as though chased by an avalanche. Meanwhile, all the telephoto lenses film him, since Coco is now a celebrity in Mexico. They have dedicated a documentary to him, produced by Wipeout Project, which tells of his exploits but also of his daily life, and is also about three other surfers and extreme sports lovers: Moisés Landa, otherwise known as El Flaco, the lean one, Oscar Moncada and David Rutherford.

I wonder how many more years it will be before the next big wave in front of Ensenada – who knows what Coco Nogales will be doing that day.

18

La Ruta del Vino

A FEW KILOMETRES NORTH OF ENSENADA, at El Sauzal, the México 3 branches off, and leaving the coast, goes towards Tecate, the birthplace of the beer of the same name, which is known throughout the entire Republic. Prior to that, however, in the Guadelupe valley, we witness the triumph of wine producers: all Mexican wine – or, at least, any worth mentioning – is produced here. Perhaps the owners of the vineyards that stretch as far as the eye can see in Baja's one and only bright green area do not remember that all this wealth has roots in the stubbornness of those Jesuits who planted California's first vines. In Alta, which has belonged to the US for the past century and a half, wines compete with European wines the world over and even restrict their import on American soil. The bottles of Chardonnay and Cabernet Sauvignon from Baja put up a good fight on the market, especially internally. The eminent wine expert, Émile Peynaud from Bordeaux, goes as far as claiming that the Calafia vineyards, in the heart of the valley, produce the best grapes in the world. I have no way of verifying what his fellow-Frenchmen think about that, but frankly, I think he exaggerates. Yet the fact remains that in recent decades the quality has become increasingly refined, and nowadays established producers like Domecq, LA, Cetto or Santo Tomás, offer more than respectable wines. Perhaps they are a little too full-bodied and high in alcohol content for our demanding palates – let's just say that it's hard to convince me that Mexican wine is preferable to the large variety of excellent beers available (now they definitely can score points against all their European equivalents) – but they are certainly able to make me forget the sour taste of the Padre Kino I reluctantly tried 25 years ago, during my first visits to Mexico. Then, I had embraced beer without looking back. Now, however, in Valle de Guadalupe, when I try the wine in producers' *bodegas* (wine cellars), I think differently and appreciate the results.

If the Jesuits are now a distant memory, we too have almost forgotten to what we owe the existence of present vineyards. Without these sturdy vines that take root in sandy soil and enjoy the Pacific breeze, we would have no wine in Europe. That is because the story of the vine lists one death through an epidemic and one resurrection. And this resurrection took place thanks to both Californias and to Chile.

It was a steamer that spread the 'plague'. In 1869, on the French coast, from some hold or other disembarked, amongst others, a tiny, almost invisible little insect, like a louse or an aphid. This phylloxera, an American creature which had not been able to cause much damage to the vines brought over by the Conquistadors thanks to the sandy soil that protected and strengthened their roots, became a plague in Europe, causing a shortage, corroding the roots and killing off all the vineyards, starting from France but then spreading across the rest of the Continent. No poison could overcome it. Within just a few years, many original vines had disappeared forever. In Italy, the phylloxera plague arrived later, but with equally devastating results. Wine seemed doomed to become no more than a memory. Luckily, the French discovered a cure: the vine would travel backwards; in other terms, they would import the roots from Chile and California, where the plants had developed defences that made them immune to the phylloxera. Therefore, these vines, the descendants of which, 3 or 4 centuries earlier, had crossed the Atlantic aboard caravels and galleons, would give their ancestors a new lease of life. From that moment on, all European wines would come from American vines. If vine growing still exists in the Old World, we owe it all to immigrants and Jesuit missionaries, who stubbornly planted them on the other side of the ocean, thus creating not only a precious 'reserve' but one that was more resistant and immune to the phylloxera.

19

Frontera

TECATE DOES NOT FEEL like a soulless place on the border but rather a peaceful town that lives around its large beer factory. This is where the first ever canned beer was produced (the habit is to squeeze half a lemon and add a pinch of salt before pulling up the ring: this is done both for the taste and in order to disinfect the edge of the can), as well as Carta Blanca, which is perhaps not as good as the others but decent enough. We head west along the Federal 2, which leads to Mexicali, away from Tijuana which I shall not be seeing this time, but which I already know.

It is still not clear why the world's busiest border town is called that. The first time it appeared under the name of Tía Juana was in 1809, when a San Diego missionary christened a 50 year-old Indio and recorded him in the register as being from the village of 'La Tía Juana'. Who this 'Auntie Joan' was remains a mystery. There is a legend about an influential lady of the area, but in fact the friar had hispanised a native term, which sounded something like 'Latijuan'. Already, back at the start of the 18th century, there was a village in the south of the peninsula called San Andrés Tiguana. Perhaps a missionary or a Spanish soldier returning to San Diego had decided to use the same name for a new settlement that was growing further north. In any case, in the 19th century, the city was known as Tía Juana, and when the United States appropriated half of Mexico, the peninsula of Baja California managed to hold on to Tijuana just to keep a land connection with the rest of the nation. At the time, it was little more than a group of scattered huts, but it grew fast thanks to the customs house. In 1911, the anarchic wing of the revolution, which was chiefly inspired by Ricardo Flores Magón, turned Baja California into its battleground. They kept hold of Tijuana for a few months before being defeated by Porfirio Díaz's army. Villa and Zapata were far away, as was the dream of a peninsula run according to the principles of anarchy. So the insurgents found themselves wrongly accused by the central government of wanting to separate Baja California from the rest of the country. It is hard to imagine that the United States' most treasured border spot could have become the capital of 'subversives'. Instead, in the Twenties, it became the capital of drunken gringos, who would come down here to bite their thumbs at Prohibitionism. Hollywood was nearby, and at night, along the dusty streets of Tía Juana, would prance the tall and rowdy figures of Douglas Fairbanks Jr, Clark Gable and Bing Crosby. Even Al Capone came here, but he took care never to be seen in public with as much as one hair out of place. No doubt Rita Hayworth attracted far more attention than he did; she often sang at the Riorita, one of that bygone era's old clubs.

Starting from the Forties, the population has been growing faster than the federal capital and Tijuana has become three separate cities. First, there is the city of tourists down from the wealthy north, full of large hotels with lounges for wild and unruly parties, glittering shopping centres, trendy restaurants and a luxuriantly green golf club that sucks up a large proportion of the water which is in short supply for many others. Then, there is the city of the original inhabitants, who are increasingly bewildered by the whirl of traumatic changes. Finally, there is the built-up area of *maquiladoras*, foreign textile factories that attract hordes of Mexicans from the rest of the country. Many of these arrive in the hope of passing over 'to the other side', but this is a difficult dream to achieve, and so they stop here to earn low wages with fast-paced, repetitive jobs – where no one so much as dares mention union rights. Meanwhile, on 'the other side', they have erected a wall that melts into the Pacific, although barbed wire and border patrol cannot keep back all those who, every day – and especially every night – attempt to pass across by inventing thousands of different methods, including digging tunnels.

The Carretera Federal 2 follows along the border for a while, descends towards El Cóndor, then rises again at La Rumorosa – which poet Carlos Pellicer described as being 'eternity cloaked in gold' – where the wide carriageway shrinks to a mountain road that runs past several canyons – Los Llanos, Los Muertos, La Guadalupe – before finally becoming the wide and straight México 2D that flanks the merciless Laguna Salada desert. There, the blinding whiteness is salt, which in the heat, forms evanescent and blurred mirages and gives the impression of an expanse of snow. The ardent air vibrates so much that, from afar, even the carcass of a rusty van looks like a house, and were we on foot like those poor Chinese a century ago, we would imagine that we had found a little water and a welcoming home that would mean we were safe.

Some people still call this spot El Desierto de los Chinos. In the 19th century, thousands of Chinese emigrated to Mexico, in order to work on the emerging railways. You could not see a railway without scores of black-clad Chinese concentrating on laying tracks, tightening bolts on sleepers, and levelling out the ground with pickaxes. In photos taken at the time, they look like an army of ants. In 1900, a large group of Cantonese settled in Mazatlán, on the continent, along the same parallel as Cabo San Lucas. Work was scarce and they went towards Guaymas, an 800-kilometre stretch, on carts, mules or on foot. It was an exodus where many died as a result of the varied hardships. Since they did not find work in Guaymas either, it is a wonder they imagined there would be something for them on the other side of the gulf; but they nevertheless embarked on a steamboat bound for San Felipe in Baja California Norte and travelled across the Sea of Cortez. However, San Felipe was no more than a fishing village – the umpteenth chimera. A few Chinese were lured by a certain José Escobedo. He claimed that, in the growing town of Mexicali, 200 kilometres further north, a workforce was needed to dig irrigation canals. The Chinese had little choice, so they followed the man, like so many Mexicans nowadays who give money to coyotes or *polleros*, human traffickers who take desperate people over the border and often let them die in the desert. José Escobedo extracted $100 from 43 Chinese ready to follow him. This was not done in bad faith, since he did go with them, assuring them that he knew where to stock up on water along the way.

It was August in 1902, when temperatures in Laguna Salada exceed 50 degrees. On top of that, the Chinese were all dressed in black, which attracted the rays of the sun implacably, and many were barefoot or wore those canvas slippers which were torn to shreds within just hours. They had to keep drinking water in order not to get dehydrated, and the insufficient reserves of water were quickly exhausted. The first man died after 30 kilometres. In Tres Pozos, where Escobedo was certain he would quench his thirst, water was just a mirage: something that looked like a lake but was actually salt mixed with soil, which the heat had caused to vibrate and seem liquid. It was the same picture at every stop: not a trace of the water promised by Escobado, and more Chinese dying. Nine days later, the Mexican managed to reach the waters of Río Hardy, a tributary of the Colorado. The six surviving Chinese out of the original 43 who had left San Felipe no longer had the strength to celebrate their safety. And Mexicali, the 'promised land', was still very far.

On the other side of the *frontera*, there is Mexico's twin, Calexico, and you can tell by the names of these places that they have been invented recently: Cal-exico, or California-Mexico; Mexi-cali, or Mexico-California. The capital of Baja Norte, Mexicali is the site of an excellent university, as well as a centre of thriving commerce with the neighbouring North. It owes its prosperity to the vast plain at the mouth of the Colorado, which, thanks to irrigation canals – that much yearned-for goal of the Chinese – has developed into the peninsula's most fertile agricultural area. In truth, nowadays the Colorado is reduced to very small streams because almost all its abundant water is tapped by American dams and farming canals. So far, all the Mexican protests against the exploitation of a river which, on this side of the border, is no more than a distant memory, have had little success. Federico Fellini got a totally different impression of it when in 1985 he ventured here while chasing the dream of a film that was never realised. This is what he wrote in his director's Block-Notes:

'The first town over the border is Mexicali, which is a picture of desolation and ruin. Dilapidated houses, ravaged streets, detritus, men sitting on the pavement wrapped in their cloaks and closed off in sleepy abandonment. It's the anthropologist who decided we should spend the night here, partly to get in touch with a certain Silvio, who possesses extraordinary powers.'

The 'anthropologist' was Carlos Castaneda, author of books such as *The Teachings of Don Juan: A Yaqui Way of Knowledge*, *Journey to Ixtlan* and *A Separate Reality*, which were very popular in the Seventies and Eighties among those who went to Mexico in search of a kind of affordable spirituality and 'magic', as an alternative to the hyped-up East, particularly India. Fellini had been trying to contact Castaneda for years, and was cherishing a plan to make a film based on his books, since he was attracted by the 'separate realities' which the mysterious writer seemed to know about in great depth. When he finally managed to arrange a meeting in Los Angeles, the two of them, together with an escort, their constant companion Pietro Notarianni, friend and collaborator on every one of Fellini's film projects – undertook a long journey across Mexico to see if, along the way, they could draft a screenplay and find the right setting, characters and sensations. The journey was 'long' for Fellini, who would have gone as far as Yucatán with his people, but not for Castaneda, who, when he became aware of a 'presence' – Fellini calls it 'The Voice' in his notes – which described the 'anthropologist' as a rascal and recommended that the director not trust him, vanished one night from the motel where they were staying. It appears that Fellini and Castaneda never met after that, and that every attempt on the part of the director to get back in contact was met with complete silence. Now that they have both passed on to other dimensions, in 'separate' realities, – who knows? – perhaps they have managed to clear things up about that journey which was, in many ways, worrying if not 'illuminating' ...

Perhaps Mexicali made that impression of desolation on Fellini because he arrived there at night, and also because, 20 years ago, it was less welcoming than it is now. The writer Gabriel Trujillo Muñoz, who teaches at the Universidad Autónoma de Baja California, lives here, and I have had the pleasure of translating his *El Festin De Los Cuervos*. The volume is a collection of five stories about his favourite character, the lawyer Miguel Ángel Morgado, a border Don Quixote, tireless defender of human rights and member of Amnesty International. He is relaxed and pessimistic but always ready to throw himself into misadventures, shoulder-to-shoulder with every sort of underdog, against opponents that are often as evanescent as desert mirages: small time drug traffickers, organ harvesters, both enthusiastically corrupt and unwaveringly honest policemen, abductors, bands of terrible motorcycle riders who at the same time form associations of volunteers, ex-guerrilla fighters engaged in 'mutual assistance', despicable politicians and criminals 'worthy of respect', gamblers and prostitutes. A mishmash in which Morgado functions skilfully, conscious that justice has no place in this world but that to give up its pursuit would be unworthy of someone who, like he, is Mexican down to the bone.

I asked Gabriel Trujillo Muñoz to tell me what it is like to live two steps away – in fact, *a dos cuadras,* two blocks, as his poem says – from the border *par excellence*. In answer to me, he printed out something he had written some time earlier and gave it to me. 'Here, this is where I've tried to say what it's like.'

And so I will translate.

'The border has shaped me from my very childhood and continues to teach me even now I am past fifty. The first thing you learn is to lay aside the stereotypes which so many travellers, both Mexican and foreign, have created while passing through this part of the world. Living day after day with another person, with other people who, when all is said and done, are a part of you, is an enlightening experience. There are two reasons for this: because it allows us to see clearly that the border, no matter how much wire netting and how many trenches are built, always ends up uniting rather than separating those who live in its shadow. The image of a terrible and violent border is as truthful as the reality of a border made with joint labour and a spirit of sacrifice. The *fronterizo*, be he Mexican, Chicano or from the United States, whether he be Chinese, Japanese or Korean, knows that a shared effort builds an unbreakable bond that transcends judgement and prejudice. Moreover, on the other hand, it is an enlightening experience because, for those who live it day after day, the border is an ongoing life lesson and an example of obstinacy and endurance. Perhaps this is because the border on which I live is an endless expanse of sand, a hard and hostile land, but which simultaneously fills your soul with its nature that is alive and tenacious, and its transparent light which soothes your pain.

The border on which I live and work is made up of barbed wire and a wall of disconnected metal plates, a market of second-hand goods and a city like Mexicali, which grows in the middle of the desert, like a mirage. A mirage that does not recall the wonders of a tale from the *Thousand and One Nights* but a mutant monster of our own, emerging from a cheap science fiction film like Ed Wood's. The most representative image of the border nowadays is the long line of vehicles and people waiting to cross over to the other side, into the green dollar paradise. And what is 'the other side' for a *fronterizo*? Certainly not Disneyland, Hollywood or Las Vegas, but something more modest: the other side of our own reality, a reality made up of rural people, of flat horizons as far as the eye can see, cultivated fields and shopping centres, where Spanish is spoken rather than English. And that is why the border is so much more than a line surveyed by remote control aeroplanes and *migra* (border control) patrols and a tunnel for smuggling drugs and shootings among narcos. It is much more than migrants drowning in the canals to which the Río Colorado has been reduced, or the dead dehydrated between the desert dunes, under the implacable sun of our eternal summer.

So then what is the border for a *fronterizo* like myself?

It is a way of seeing others without the aura of legend, of accepting that the landscape is a vital part of our collective existence; that certain classic Western film images have not disappeared from the world scene because, at every sunset, I can admire them in the splendour of nature ablaze; that the clash between two cultures, Latin American and Anglo-Saxon, can trigger sparks of violence and intolerance but also spark off the imagination of their artists.

Thinking about it, I believe that my vision of the border derives from the fact that my parents, who were born much further south, in Michoacán and Jalisco, despite having the opportunity to emigrate to the United States, chose to stay in Mexicali, on the Mexican side of the border, where they fulfilled their own destiny: a destiny that has also become mine. I remember one of my mother's sisters who would come and visit us, who lived in Los Angeles and who would always arrive at our house with lots of presents and tell us how good life was on the other side. However, after preparing her typical Jalisco dishes, which she devoured in one go, my mother would respond with total confidence, "Thank you, but we're fine here."

And it is the same thing I say now: I am fascinated by the border as it allows me to see the lights and the shadows of the American Empire, but I like to see them from this side of the line, from this country of mine that is so full of cracks and always on the point of breaking into pieces and which, in spite of everything, still manages to remain on its feet and go forward. Just like my parents, I declare that despite all the difficulties, this is where I want to stay. In this No Man's Land, in this place of transition and permanence, where nomads and settlers live alongside one another. Or, even better: where the nomad and the settler we all carry inside co-exist.'

20

Colorado, *el río Desaparecido*

WE COULD NOT LEAVE BAJA without an excursion to what remains of the Colorado. That is what Father Kino called it, and in Spanish it means 'red' because even the small amount of water that still reaches the Gulf of California carries a rusty silt, a deep red which during the time of the Jesuit explorers – 1701 – must have been an overwhelming spectacle. Back then, the power of the Colorado would clash with the strong tides, and walls of water would form which would sweep across the plains and then return, with equally devastating effect, in an endless struggle between the red river and the vermillion sea – a clash of Titans. The Colorado, which springs from the Rocky Mountains about 23,000 kilometres away from here, is still impetuous while crossing canyons in a tortuous route that runs from the state of the same name to Utah, then between Arizona and California, marking the border. However, along the way, and particularly in flat areas devoted to intensive cultivation, a host of canals bleed it dry, as well as dams generating electric power, and so at the end of its course there is a vast flood plain that extends as far as Arizona, while in the Mexican part, the delta is reduced to a cobweb of tiny streams which, when seen from an airplane, look like arterial diversions, or like huge dried up trees with branches stretched out in sand that becomes muddy around what scarce water filters down this far.

In this case, too, we have the proper musical accompaniment: *End of the Road*, by Eddie Vedder, the soundtrack of the masterpiece *Into the Wild*. Before entering Alaska, the film's protagonist travels down the Colorado in a kayak, defying the Rocky Mountain rapids, and at the end of an adventurous descent, reaches the Mexican border in Baja. He uses embittered words about those who have appropriated all the water in the north, and left nothing but this desolate, muddy, barren estuary. Still, if you think about it, this is not an evil: the Colorado gathers tons of pesticides, fertilisers and industrial waste. If it flowed into the gulf with that load of poison, the northern areas of the Sea of Cortez would be a graveyard. As it is, with all the muddy, reddish water, the survival of the vaquita (porpoise) is still under threat; it is the Gulf's Phocoena Sinus, the shyest, most reserved, most delicate cetacean and extremely sensitive to the ecosystem's variations. So let them keep their water of ill omen.

EDDIE VEDDER is singing *End of the Road*. It is the end of the road. We return to Mexicali to catch a plane. As usual, before leaving Mexico, I recall the words of Pablo Neruda:

Mexico,
You have opened your doors and your hands
to the wanderer and the wounded,
to the exiled and the hero.
I feel this could not be said otherwise and I want
my words to settle, one more time,
like kisses upon your walls.
Like an equal, you have opened your war gate
and your mane filled with the sons of strangers
and you have placed your rough hands
on the cheeks of every son
ever since the torment of the world gave birth to you
    amid tears. Here will I stop,

Mexico,
here will I leave this writing
on your temples, so that age
may wipe out this new discourse
by one who loved you because you are free and
    profound. I say farewell but I am not leaving
I am leaving but I cannot say farewell to you.

I will come back to this strip of desert that stretches into the sea. I will come back to Baja to feel, once again, the unequalled thrill of seeing the whales. And even if I am unable to explain the reason for this state of mind that touches on emotion and tickles my heart, I really think they know it. Yes. The whales know.

Translator's Note

Translating *Le balene lo sanno* into *The Whales Know* has been a joy and a privilege. I wish to express my heartfelt thanks to the author, Pino Cacucci, for being so approachable, helpful and appreciative. I would also like to thank Sue Cumisky, Howard Curtis and Christopher Parker for their kind, invaluable advice and support, whilst I was working on this translation.

Katherine Gregor

ALSO PUBLISHED IN
THE LITERARY TRAVELLER SERIES

PINO CACUCCI was born in 1955 in Alessandria, Piedmont, and grew up in Chiavari, Italy. In the early Eighties he spent long periods in Paris and Barcelona, and subsequently made his first trips to Mexico and Central America, where he resided for some years. He is a prolific translator from Spanish, and has written over 20 works of fiction and non-fiction, for which he has won over 16 awards, including the *Pluma de Plata Mexicana* in 1992 and 1997 for the best foreign writing on Mexico.